THE
PRESIDENTS
OF THE UNITED STATES

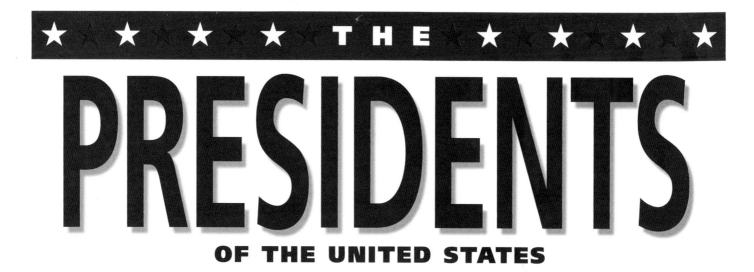

THE
PRESIDENTS
OF THE UNITED STATES

SIMON ADAMS

PRINCETON ▪ LONDON

www.two-canpublishing.com

Published in the United States and Canada by
Two-Can Publishing LLC
234 Nassau Street
Princeton, NJ 08542

For more information on Two-Can books and multimedia,
call 1-609-921-6700, fax 1-609-921-3349, or visit our
Web site at http://www.two-canpublishing.com

Created for Two-Can by

Picthall & Gunzi Ltd

21A Widmore Road, Bromley, Kent BR1 1RW, England
Tel: (0)20 8460 4032 Fax: (0)20 8460 4021

Editor Lauren Robertson   **DTP designer** Anthony Cutting
Editorial director Christiane Gunzi   **Senior designer** Dominic Zwemmer
Picture researchers Louise Thomas (ilumi) and Julia Harris-Voss
Indexer Jillian Somerscales

"Two-Can" is a trademark of Two-Can Publishing
Two-Can publishing is a division of Zenith Entertainment Ltd,
43–45 Dorset Street, London W1U 7NA, England

ISBN 1–58728–0922
ISBN 1–58728–0930

HC   2 3 4 5 6 7 8 9 10 02
PC   2 3 4 5 6 7 8 9 10 02

Printed by Phoenix Color, USA
Color reproduction by Next Century Ltd, Hong Kong

Words in **bold** in the text can be found in the glossary at the back of the book

CONTENTS

WHAT IS A PRESIDENT?

The president of the United States of America is probably the most powerful person in the world. He is the leader of the US, which is the world's richest and strongest country. The US president is a figure of world importance. So, who is the president, and what exactly does he do?

WHY HAVE A PRESIDENT?

When the US won its independence from Britain in 1783, the leaders of the new country sat down to write the laws on how the country would be governed. This became the US **Constitution**. The US leaders did not want America to have a royal family and decided that the country should be a **republic**, which means it is led by an elected head of state or president. The first president – George Washington – took office in 1789.

WHO CAN BE PRESIDENT?

The president must be at least 35 years old, must have been born in the US and must have lived in the country for at least 14 years. Both men and women can be president, but, so far, the presidents have all been male. He or she cannot serve more than two terms as president, which is a total of eight years.

WHAT DOES THE PRESIDENT DO?

The president's main duty is to protect the Constitution and to uphold the laws passed by **Congress**, the legislative, or law-making, body of the USA. It is made up of the lower **House of Representatives** and the upper **Senate**. All members of the House and one third of the Senate members are elected every two years. To help run the government, the president points a team of politicians called a **Cabinet**, and ne has to be approved by Congress.

sident can recommend new laws to Congress.
gestion for a new rule – is prepared by
r other members of the Cabinet. The
o, or stop, a bill becoming an act,
can be overturned by Congress.
dent and his team run the different
f state and make sure that the
ns of the country are upheld.

HOW IS THE PRESIDENT ELECTED?

The president is elected through a system known as the **Electoral College**. Every four years, Americans choose their state's Electors – Electoral College members – at the polls. Each state has a College membership equal to its total number of representatives in Congress. Everyone votes for a list of Electors that belongs to their chosen party – **Democratic**, **Republican**, or **Independent**. The winning party list of people for each state then meets and casts its total vote for its own party's presidential and vice-presidential candidate. Each state then sends its votes to Congress, which adds the results together from all 50 states and declares a winner. The total number of electors in the Electoral College is 538, so a presidential candidate needs 270 votes to win. Many people dislike this system because a president can be elected with a majority of votes in the College, even if he or she fails to get a majority of the people's votes in the country.

HOW POWERFUL IS A PRESIDENT?

The president runs the administration of the country. His powers are limited by the Constitution through a system known as "the separation of powers." The president is held in check by the **judiciary**, which is led by the US Supreme Court, and by Congress.

▲ First Lady Eleanor Roosevelt was one of the few first ladies who have made their own important mark on the world.

5

▲ The Oval Office inside the White House where the president spends most of his time and makes his decisions.

The idea is that each of these three (the president, the judiciary, and Congress) can keep a check, or balance, on the other two to make sure that one does not get too powerful. But the president still has a lot of power:

• He is commander-in-chief of the armed forces and makes decisions on defense. In times of war, he is often given great powers by Congress.

• He oversees relations with other countries. He meets world leaders, appoints **ambassadors**, negotiates **treaties** and agreements, attends international conferences, and represents the USA on foreign visits.

• He leads the country. He sends new bills to Congress for approval and sets out the budget, a financial plan which raises **taxes** to pay for the government and the running of the country. He influences the conduct of government through the appointment of ministers and officials, and acts as a figurehead at times of national success or tragedy. A strong president can change the history of the world and make a huge impression on the daily lives of every American, like Franklin Roosevelt did during the Great Depression and World War II.

WHO IS THE FIRST LADY?

The wife of the president is given the title of First Lady during her husband's term in office. She is not elected and she holds no power of her own, but she can influence events by showing an interest in and campaigning for particular issues.

The first First Lady to make her mark on history was Eleanor Roosevelt, the wife of Franklin Roosevelt, who campaigned for social justice and human rights. Hillary Clinton is the most recent First Lady to be powerful in her own right and to support and work for major issues.

WHO IS THE VICE-PRESIDENT?

From 1789–1804, the person who was runner-up in the presidential election was appointed **vice-president**. This caused great problems, though, because the president and vice-president sometimes came from different political parties with different views and policies, so the system was changed. Today, the president's **running mate** now becomes vice-president. This means that he or she is chosen by the president, and is elected to office at the same time. Part of the vice-president's job is as Speaker of the **Senate**, but otherwise he or she has few formal powers. The vice-president is part of the Cabinet and is often used by the president for special tasks, such as generating support on a particular issue. If the president dies, or resigns, or is removed from office, the vice-president takes over as president, and appoints a new vice-president.

WHERE DOES THE PRESIDENT LIVE?

The president lives in the capital city at the White House, 1600 Pennsylvania Avenue, Washington, D.C. Officially known as the Executive Mansion, the White House serves both as a home for the president and his family, and as the office of the presidency. Here, the president holds Cabinet sessions and other meetings, and entertains heads of state and important visitors to the US. The president's personal office is known as the Oval Office, because of its shape. The president can also use Camp David, which is a country home in Maryland, some 68 miles (110km) from the White House.

The US capital city is named after the first president, George Washington, and is unique because it is not part of a state. It is a federal district, the District of Columbia (D.C.), and has its own mayor and a city council. It has no **senators** and it sends only one non-voting **delegate** to the House of Representatives.

▶ Four presidents have been assassinated, including John F. Kennedy, in 1963.

PRESIDENTS OF THE USA

In 212 years there have been 43 US presidents, from George Washington in 1789 to George W Bush in 2001. So far, all of them have been men. One president, Grover Cleveland, served two separate terms. Four presidents, namely Abraham Lincoln, James Garfield, William McKinley, and John Kennedy, were assassinated in office. Another four – Benjamin Harrison, Zachary Taylor, Warren Harding, and Franklin Roosevelt – died in office. One president, Richard Nixon, was forced to resign. The ages of the presidents when they came to office range from Theodore Roosevelt at 42 to Ronald Reagan at 69, and their terms in office from a brief 31 days by William Harrison to the lengthy 12 years of Franklin Roosevelt. Some, like George Washington, Abraham Lincoln, and Franklin Roosevelt, have left a powerful mark on history, while others are remembered as failures. Each one tried to govern well and has contributed to the history of the USA.

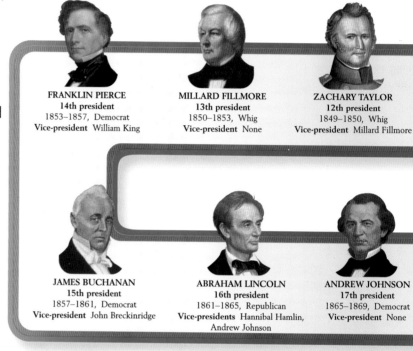

FRANKLIN PIERCE
14th president
1853–1857, Democrat
Vice-president William King

MILLARD FILLMORE
13th president
1850–1853, Whig
Vice-president None

ZACHARY TAYLOR
12th president
1849–1850, Whig
Vice-president Millard Fillmore

JAMES BUCHANAN
15th president
1857–1861, Democrat
Vice-president John Breckinridge

ABRAHAM LINCOLN
16th president
1861–1865, Republican
Vice-presidents Hannibal Hamlin,
Andrew Johnson

ANDREW JOHNSON
17th president
1865–1869, Democrat
Vice-president None

DWIGHT EISENHOWER
34th president
1953–1961, Republican
Vice-president Richard Nixon

HARRY TRUMAN
33rd president
1945–1953, Democrat
Vice-president Alben Barkley

FRANKLIN ROOSEVELT
32nd president
1933–1945, Democrat
Vice-presidents John Garner,
Henry Wallace, Harry Truman

HERBERT HOOVER
31st president
1929–1933, Republican
Vice-president Charles Curtis

CALVIN COOLIDGE
30th president
1923–1929, Republican
Vice-president Charles Dawes

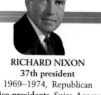

JOHN KENNEDY
35th president
1961–1963, Democrat
Vice-president Lyndon Johnson

LYNDON JOHNSON
36th president
1963–1969, Democrat
Vice-president Hubert Humphrey

RICHARD NIXON
37th president
1969–1974, Republican
Vice-presidents Spiro Agnew,
Gerald Ford

GERALD FORD
38th president
1974–1977, Republican
Vice-president Nelson Rockefeller

JAMES CARTER
39th president
1977–1981, Democrat
Vice-president Walter Mondale

GEORGE WASHINGTON
1st president
1789–1797, Federalist
Vice-president John Adams

JOHN ADAMS
2nd president
1797–1801, Federalist
Vice-president Thomas Jefferson

THOMAS JEFFERSON
3rd president
1801–1809, Democratic-Republican
Vice-presidents Aaron Burr,
George Clinton

JAMES MADISON
4th president
1809–1817, Democratic-Republican
Vice-presidents George Clinton,
Elbridge Gerry

JAMES MONROE
5th president
1817–1825 Democratic-Republican
Vice-president Daniel Tompkins

JAMES POLK
11th president
1845–1849, Democrat
Vice-president George Dallas

JOHN TYLER
10th president
1841–1845, Whig
Vice-president None

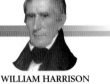

WILLIAM HARRISON
9th president
1841, Whig
Vice-president John Tyler

MARTIN VAN BUREN
8th president
1837–1841, Democrat
Vice-president Richard Johnson

ANDREW JACKSON
7th president
1829–1837, Democrat
Vice-presidents John Calhoun,
Martin Van Buren

JOHN Q ADAMS
6th president
1825–1829 Democratic-Republican
Vice-president John Calhoun

ULYSSES GRANT
18th president
1869–1877, Republican
Vice-presidents Schuyler Colfax;
Henry Wilson

RUTHERFORD HAYES
19th president
1877–1881, Republican
Vice-president William Wheeler

JAMES GARFIELD
20th president
1881, Republican
Vice-president Chester Arthur

CHESTER ARTHUR
21st president
1881–1885, Republican
Vice-president None

GROVER CLEVELAND
22nd president
1885–1889, Democrat
Vice-president Thomas Hendricks

BENJAMIN HARRISON
23rd president
1889–1893, Republican
Vice-president Levi Morton

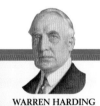

WARREN HARDING
29th president
1921–1923, Republican
Vice-president Calvin Coolidge

WOODROW WILSON
28th president
1913–1921, Democrat
Vice-president Thomas Marshall

WILLIAM TAFT
27th president
1909–1913, Republican
Vice-president James Sherman

THEODORE ROOSEVELT
26th president
1901–1909, Republican
Vice-president Charles Fairbanks

WILLIAM McKINLEY
25th president
1897–1901, Republican
Vice-presidents Garret Hobart,
Theodore Roosevelt

GROVER CLEVELAND
24th president
1893–1897, Democrat
Vice-president Adlai Stevenson

RONALD REAGAN
40th president
1981–1989, Republican
Vice-president George Bush

GEORGE BUSH
41st president
1989–1993, Republican
Vice-president Dan Quayle

WILLIAM CLINTON
42nd president
1993–2001, Democrat
Vice-president Al Gore

GEORGE W BUSH
43rd president
2001– Republican
Vice-president Dick Cheney

DEATH DATES
Three of the first five presidents – Thomas Jefferson, John Adams, and James Monroe – died on July 4, Independence Day!

GEORGE WASHINGTON

☆ **TERM**
1789–1797

☆ **PARTY**
Federalist

☆ **VICE-PRESIDENT**
John Adams

☆ **FIRST LADY**
Martha Dandridge Custis

☆ **STATES IN THE UNION** *16*

> *I hope I shall always possess firmness and virtue enough to maintain the character of an Honest Man.*

GEORGE WASHINGTON, 1788

TOOTHLESS WONDER
Washington rarely smiled in public because he had false teeth, made out of ivory and other materials.

George Washington was born into a wealthy family in Westmoreland County, Virginia, in 1732.

His father was a trader, planter, and iron mill operator, and George spent his childhood enjoying the land – hunting, fishing, riding, and boating.

▶ The birthplace of George Washington in Wakefield, Virginia.

EARLY LIFE

At the age of 15, Washington left school wanting to join the British Royal Navy (Virginia was a British colony). His widowed mother refused to let him go to sea, so he trained as a surveyor, mapping the uncharted lands to the west of Virginia. In 1753 he joined the local **militia** and fought for the British, gaining valuable experience of military life. He also became a member of the Virginia **legislature**, but he made little impression on state politics. As a farmer, he was far more interested in his estate at Mount Vernon, which he had inherited from his half-brother, Lawrence.

1732
Born in Virginia

1747
Leaves school and trains as a surveyor

1753
Joins Virginia militia and fights for the British against the French

1758
Enters politics in Virginia

1761
Marries Martha Dandridge Custis, a wealthy widow

1775–81
Revolutionary War against Britain

CROSSING THE DELAWARE

⭐ On Christmas night 1776, Washington took his 2,400 troops across the ice-bound Delaware River and surprised the German troops who were fighting for the British and were camped on the other side. His success at this battle – the Battle of Trenton – made him a national hero and helped the Americans to win victory over the British in 1781.

Crossing the Delaware

INTO WAR

During the 1760s and early 1770s, relations between Britain and its 13 American colonies grew steadily worse. Fighting broke out in 1775 and, a year later, the colonies declared their independence. Washington, as commander-in-chief of the **Colonial Army**, was a strong leader who inspired great loyalty among his troops. The British soldiers were successful at first, but Washington gradually won the upper hand. By 1781 the British were defeated, and America was free.

After the war, Washington returned to his family home in Mount Vernon to farm.

In 1787, however, he was summoned to attend the **Constitutional Convention** in Philadelphia, which was putting together the **Constitution** that would govern the new country. He was elected president of the convention, so he was the natural choice to become the first president of the United States of America in 1789.

MR. PRESIDENT

For the first four years of his presidency, George Washington was busy setting up the new country. Among other things, he had to create a legal system, set **taxes**, and establish a capital city. He wanted to retire after one term, but he was persuaded to continue. War between Britain and France, attacks on US shipping, and political problems at home made his last years as president unhappy ones.

Surprisingly, Washington was shy and modest, and he disliked public speaking and formal occasions. Although he was not an ambitious man, his strong sense of duty and his willingness to volunteer for public service made him a fine president. In 1797 he finally retired to his beloved Mount Vernon. When he died in 1799, George Washington, first president of the USA, was mourned across America as a brave soldier and a strong leader – truly the father of his country.

HONEST GEORGE

⭐ As a child, George Washington cut down a cherry tree on his father's farm with an axe that was given to him as a present. He owned up with the words: "I can't tell a lie, Pa; you know I can't tell a lie."

1775
Commander-in-chief of the Colonial Army

1787
Helps write US Constitution

1789
Elected first president of the USA

1792
Re-elected for a second term

1797
Retires as president

1799
Dies at Mount Vernon, Virginia

▶ The Inauguration of George Washington, first president of the United States of America.

1735
Born in Braintree,
Massachusetts

1755
Graduates from
Harvard University

1758
Becomes
a lawyer

1776
Seconds the motion in
favor of independence

◀ Birthplace of John Adams
in Braintree, Massachusetts

John Adams, who was born in Braintree (now Quincy), Massachusetts, was a bright and able student. He went to Harvard University and became a lawyer, then used his knowledge of law to enter politics. Adams soon became a revolutionary and took part in anti-British campaigns. He also wrote pamphlets against Stamp Duty, a special **tax** that was imposed on America by the British in 1765. This duty meant that taxes had to be paid on legal documents, newspapers, and other printed papers.

In 1774 Adams became a member of the **Continental Congress**. He supported the **motion** in favor of independence and helped Thomas Jefferson to write the **Declaration of Independence**. Adams also proposed that George Washington should be leader of the **Colonial Army**. As a result of his high profile, Adams became **ambassador** to France in 1777. He was not successful as a **diplomat** and in 1782 returned home, where he played an important part in negotiating the peace **treaty**

☆ **TERM**
1797–1801

☆ **PARTY**
Federalist

☆ **VICE-PRESIDENT**
Thomas Jefferson

☆ **FIRST LADY**
Abigail Smith

☆ **STATES IN THE UNION** *16*

2nd president

JOHN ADAMS

No man who ever held the office of president would congratulate a friend on obtaining it.

JOHN ADAMS, 1824

FAT ADAMS
John Adams ate so much that his enemies began to call him 'His Rotundity' and even his wife said he was "so very fat."

1826
Dies in Braintree, Massachusetts

1801
Loses election to Jefferson

1796
Elected president

1776
Helps Jefferson write Declaration of Independence

1777
Envoy to France and later Britain

1783
Negotiates peace treaty with Britain

1789
Elected vice-president to George Washington

of 1783 with Britain. Adams spent another period of time as a diplomat, this time in Britain, but he was again unsuccessful, and asked if he could come home to the USA in 1788.

In 1789 President George Washington asked Adams to become his **vice-president**. He served Washington for eight years and helped to solve the arguments that broke out between the politicians of the day. When Washington stepped down as president, Adams was elected president of the US.

THE SECOND PRESIDENT

According to the laws of the day, the candidate with the second highest number of votes became vice-president. John Adams was a **Federalist**. He believed in a strong central government and by that time had become pro-Britain. His new vice-president, Thomas Jefferson, was a **Democratic-Republican**, who believed in power for individual states. He was also pro-France. Since Britain and France were at war with each other in Europe and both countries were capturing US merchant ships, it is not

MRS. ADAMS

☆ Two members of Abigail Adams' family became US presidents – her husband John in 1796 and, nearly thirty years later, their son John Quincy Adams.

Abigail Adams (formerly Smith)

very surprising that there were disagreements between Adams and Jefferson. Adams tried to keep the peace with Jefferson and worked to keep the US out of any foreign wars. He secretly sent three ambassadors to France in 1797 to draw up a treaty between the two countries. The French asked the ambassadors to bribe the French foreign minister with money in order to avoid war.

When Adams released this information to the public, war almost broke out between America and France. President Adams managed to reach an agreement with France to avoid total war, and upset his own supporters. He had already upset Jefferson by signing the *Alien and Sedition Acts*, which did not allow criticism of the government.

IN RETIREMENT

By the end of his career, John Adams was disliked by almost everyone in US politics. In 1800 he was defeated in the presidential election by Thomas Jefferson. Adams then retired to Braintree, where he lived until his death. He died 50 years from the day the Declaration of Independence was signed.

◀ In 1800 John Adams with his wife and family moved into the new official residence of the president. It later became known as the White House.

THOMAS JEFFERSON

☆ **TERM**
1801–1809

☆ **PARTY**
Democratic-Republican

☆ **VICE-PRESIDEN**
*Aaron Burr,
George Clinton*

☆ **FIRST LADY**
None

☆ **STATES IN
THE UNION** *17*

"The care of human life and happiness, and not their destruction, is the first and only legitimate object of good government."

THOMAS JEFFERSON, 1809

THE FIDDLER
Jefferson was a keen musician and played the violin for up to three hours a day. He also liked gardening and grew many exotic crops on his estate.

Thomas Jefferson has as much claim to the title of "father of his country" as George Washington because he was the author of the **Declaration of Independence** and played a major role in setting up the new country. Yet Jefferson almost failed to become president at all. Born in 1743, he was a clever man who went to college and studied philosophy and law. Then he became a lawyer, and in 1769 he became a member of the Virginia **legislature**. Jefferson strongly believed that Americans had rights that their British rulers denied them. He published anti-British leaflets to tell the American people about his beliefs.

1743
Born in Albemarle County, Virginia

1762
Graduates from College of William and Mary

1769
Enters politics in Virginia

1775
Becomes a member of the Continental Congress

1776
Drafts Declaration of Independence

1779
Becomes governor of Virginia

▶ Jefferson often entertained people at his splendid home *Monticello* in Virginia. Here he is shown hosting a Christmas party.

◄ The region called Louisiana was bought from France by the US in 1803. The area was explored by Lewis & Clark in their expedition of 1804–06. The route taken by the explorers can be seen on this map.

In 1775 Jefferson became a member of the **Continental Congress**. He almost single-handedly wrote the Declaration of Independence, the foundation of the new **republic**. During the **Revolutionary War**, he was governor of Virginia and, in 1785, he became his country's **ambassador** to France. There he saw the outbreak of the French Revolution, which he supported.

Back in the US, Jefferson joined the government as **secretary of state** but quit because of his opposition to the pro-British attitude and strong government policies of Washington's **Federalists**. Jefferson was pro-French and was against a strong federal government. His beliefs led to the birth of the first opposition party in US history – the **Democratic-Republicans**. This action started the **two-party system** that we see in government today.

EXPANDING THE COUNTRY

In 1796 Jefferson ran for president, but he was runner-up to his main rival, John Adams. As a result he became **vice-president**. In 1800 he ran for president again, but he won the same number of votes as another candidate, Aaron Burr. The **House of Representatives** considered the matter and narrowly elected Jefferson as president.

At first Jefferson was a great success. He took no notice of all the restrictions placed on his power and he made the **Louisiana Purchase** from the French, more than doubling the size of the US. Anxious to know what this new land looked like, he sent explorers Lewis and Clark on a historic, two-year expedition through this vast territory.

Jefferson was so popular that he was re-elected president in 1804, but things soon went wrong. Britain and France were at war and were attacking US shipping. President Jefferson banned all foreign trade in order to put pressure on the two countries, but the US economy suffered, and the ban was lifted before he left office in 1809.

TO MONTICELLO

On his retirement, Jefferson returned to *Monticello*, the beautiful house that he had designed and built himself. There he expanded his vast library, wrote numerous letters and books, and became a much-loved father figure until he died on July 4, 1826, the same day as his great rival, John Adams.

A GREAT DEMOCRAT

☆ In 1776 Jefferson wrote the Declaration of Independence, which is one of the greatest documents in human history. It still influences people around the world today. Jefferson also wrote books, kept a huge library, and set up the University of Virginia.

Signing the Declaration of Independence

1789
Witnesses French Revolution as ambassador

1790–93
Serves as secretary of state under Washington

1796
Elected vice-president to John Adams

1800
Elected president

1803
Buys Louisiana Territory

1809
Retires as president

1826
Dies at Monticello, Virginia

LITTLE BIG MAN
James Madison only weighed 100lbs (45kg) and his friends said he was "no bigger than a half piece of soap." His wife called him her "darling little husband."

1751
Born in Port Conway, Virginia

1771
Graduates from New Jersey College, now Princeton

1780
Elected to Continental Congress

1787
Helps draft US Constitution

1789
Elected to the House of Representatives from Virginia

1801
Becomes secretary of state under President Jefferson

Along with Washington, Adams, and Jefferson, James Madison played a vital role in establishing the newly independent United States of America. He was a clever scholar and read many books by European political thinkers. He brought their ideas to the US and put them into practice in government. Madison became a member of the **Continental Congress** in 1780. He developed the idea that governments needed to be kept under control. He believed that the three parts of government – leaders, law-makers, and judges – should be controlled by a system of "checks and balances" to stop one part getting too powerful. In this way, a strong leader could not ignore the law or the wishes of the people. These ideas were new at the time, but James Madison made sure that the US **Constitution**, which was eventually agreed in 1787, was based on this "separation of powers."

☆ **TERM**
1809–1817

☆ **PARTY**
Democratic-Republican

☆ **VICE-PRESIDENTS**
George Clinton, Elbridge Gerry

☆ **FIRST LADY**
Dorothea "Dolley" Todd

☆ **STATES IN THE UNION** *19*

4th president

JAMES MADISON

"The happy union of these states is a wonder; their Constitution a miracle; their example the hope of liberty throughout the world."

JAMES MADISON, 1829

▶ During the burning of Washington in 1814, British troops blackened the president's residence. James Madison had the building painted white to hide the marks, so it became known as the White House.

1808 Elected president	**1812** Re-elected president	**1812–15** Fights war against Britain	**1817** Retires to Virginia	**1836** Dies in Montpelier, Virginia

◀ *USS Constitution* fights the British at the outbreak of war between the two countries in 1812.

INTO OFFICE

In 1789 Madison was elected a member of the new **House of Representatives**. He became a close ally of Thomas Jefferson. When Madison left **Congress** in 1797, he fought hard against President Adams' *Alien and Sedition Acts*. Madison believed that these Acts prevented free speech. Thomas Jefferson became president in 1801 and made Madison his **secretary of state**. He served Jefferson loyally, and he was his natural successor when Jefferson stepped down. In 1808 Madison was elected as the fourth US president.

Like Jefferson before him, Madison had to deal with the problem of the war between France and Britain, and its effect on the US. Although he tried not to take sides, this proved difficult to do and, in 1812, the USA declared war on Britain to stop the country attacking US ships. The result was a disaster, as the small and badly led US forces lost battle after battle. In 1814 the British attacked the US capital, Washington, and burned it down, causing Madison's wife to flee the burning White House clutching a portrait of Washington. The US managed to win a major victory in New Orleans, which raised morale considerably. Peace was eventually declared in the US in 1815.

RETIREMENT

James Madison spent the last two years of his presidency as quite a popular president, mainly because his country was becoming more and more wealthy. He retired to Montpelier in 1817, and lived quietly in Virginia until his death in 1836.

THE STAR-SPANGLED BANNER

In September 1814, a young lawyer, Francis Key, boarded a British ship to bargain for the release of an American who was captured during the fighting between the two countries. While aboard, Key was forced to watch the British bombard a nearby fort. What he saw inspired him to write the words that became the US national anthem in 1916.

O, say can you see, by the dawn's early light,
What so proudly we hail'd at the twilight's last gleaming?
Whose broad stripes and bright stars through the perilous fight,
O'er the ramparts we watched were so gallantly streaming?
And the rockets' red glare, the bombs bursting in air,
Gave proof through the night that our flag was still there.
O, say does that star-spangled banner yet wave
O'er the land of the free, the home of the brave?

JAMES MONROE

☆ **TERM**
1817–1825

☆ **PARTY**
*Democratic-
Republican*

☆ **VICE-PRESIDENT**
Daniel Tompkins

☆ **FIRST LADY**
Elizabeth Kortright

☆ **STATES IN
THE UNION** *24*

" *The American
continents… are
henceforth not to
be considered as
subjects for future
colonization by
any European
powers.* "

JAMES MONROE, 1823

▲ The flag of 1818, when five new stars were added and there were 13 stripes (as there are today).

James Monroe was well-equipped to become a US president. He had fought in the **Revolutionary War**, and he had been a **senator**, state congressman, governor (twice), **secretary of state**, war secretary, and an **ambassador**. Above all, Monroe had been one of the two envoys who negotiated the purchase of the vast Louisiana Territory from France in 1803.

As a life-long friend of both presidents Jefferson and Madison, he was an ideal choice to succeed Madison as president in 1817.

THE PEACEMAKER

James Monroe was a great success as president. He was honest, friendly, tactful, and willing to work with both friends and opponents. He supported the pro-state, anti-big government policies of Thomas Jefferson, which meant that he was happy for the individual states to govern themselves. But he also worked well with the **Federalists**. As a result, his first term as president became known as the "Era of Good Feelings."

As president, however, Monroe faced two major problems. The first was Florida, which was owned by Spain. Members of the **Seminole Nation** who were living in Florida regularly crossed the border and raided the US. In 1818 US troops

1758
Born in Westmoreland County, Virginia

1776–80
Fights in Revolutionary War

1782
Enters politics in Virginia

1790
Elected to US Senate

1794
Acts as ambassador to France

1799
Becomes governor of Virginia

1811
Appointed secretary of state under Madison

1816
Elected president

fought back and war with Spain looked likely. In 1819 the Spanish agreed to hand over Florida, giving the US control of all the land east of the mighty Mississippi River.

The second problem that Monroe faced was **slavery**. Monroe disagreed with slavery, but he agreed with the **Missouri Compromise**, an agreement that had been worked out in **Congress**. The Compromise stated that the number of pro- and anti-slavery states in the **Union** must be the same, and this agreement lasted until the 1850s.

INTO THE HISTORY BOOKS

The one event that everyone remembers President Monroe for is the **Monroe Doctrine**, which he set out in 1823. The countries of central and southern America had gained their independence from Spain or Portugal, but the US was concerned that strong European countries, such as Britain or France, might try to take over, or colonize, these new states.

In December 1823, Monroe established a new foreign policy for the US. He stated that the US would not allow any European countries to colonize the Americas or interfere with the governing of any of its countries. The Monroe Doctrine was regularly used in the following years to protect Latin America from being taken over by the Europeans.

In 1825 James Monroe stepped down as president. He was a much-loved man and was mourned by many people when he died in 1831. Like Presidents Adams and Jefferson before him, Monroe died on July 4, Independence Day.

THE MISSOURI COMPROMISE

☆ The southern states, such as Georgia, allowed white people to keep African-American people as slaves. These slaves were made to work for no pay and were not allowed human and civil rights. Northern states, such as New York, were against slavery. By 1820 the country was split in two on this subject, as there were 11 "slave" states and 11 "free" states. In 1820 Congress agreed to let slave-owning Missouri and slave-free Maine join the Union, while slavery was still illegal in the northern part of the Louisiana Territory. A compromise was reached, and the balance between the equal numbers of pro- and anti-slavery states was maintained, but slavery continued to cause problems across the nation.

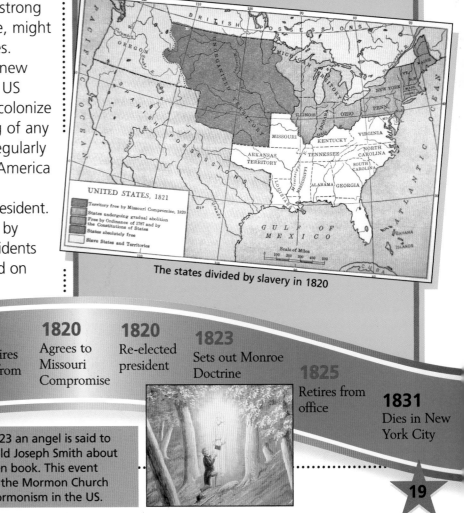

The states divided by slavery in 1820

1819 US acquires Florida from Spain

1820 Agrees to Missouri Compromise

1820 Re-elected president

1823 Sets out Monroe Doctrine

1825 Retires from office

1831 Dies in New York City

▶ In 1823 an angel is said to have told Joseph Smith about a golden book. This event started the Mormon Church and Mormonism in the US.

Florida in the 1800s

JOHN Q ADAMS

6th president

⭐ **TERM**
1825–1829

⭐ **PARTY**
Democratic-Republican

⭐ **VICE-PRESIDENT**
John Calhoun

⭐ **FIRST LADY**
Louisa Johnson

⭐ **STATES IN THE UNION** *24*

THE SNAPPER
John Quincy Adams installed the first pool table in the White House. He also kept an alligator as a pet.

> *My whole life has been a succession of disappointments. I can scarcely recollect a single instance of success.*
>
> **JOHN QUINCY ADAMS, 1820**

John Adams was very well qualified to become president. He was a gifted scholar, good at languages, and trained as a lawyer. Before becoming president, Adams was an **ambassador** to four European countries, and was a **senator** and **secretary of state**. He also negotiated the peace **treaty** with Britain that ended the 1812–15 war. In addition, his father, John Adams, was president before him, so he had trained young John for the job. Adams had even accompanied his father on **diplomatic** missions at the age of 13. But his own time as president was unsuccessful.

In the election of 1824, none of the candidates achieved a majority of votes. John Quincy Adams came second, as runner-up to Andrew Jackson. Early in 1825, the decision about who was to be president

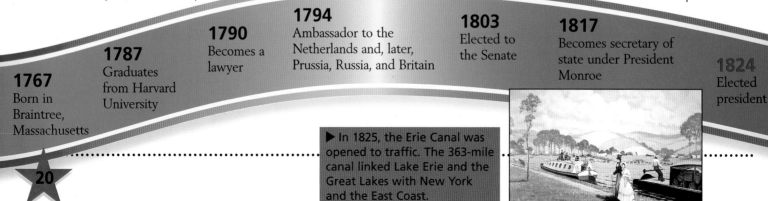

1767
Born in Braintree, Massachusetts

1787
Graduates from Harvard University

1790
Becomes a lawyer

1794
Ambassador to the Netherlands and, later, Prussia, Russia, and Britain

1803
Elected to the Senate

1817
Becomes secretary of state under President Monroe

1824
Elected president

▶ In 1825, the Erie Canal was opened to traffic. The 363-mile canal linked Lake Erie and the Great Lakes with New York and the East Coast.

went to the **House of Representatives**, where each of the 24 states had one vote. The candidate in fourth place was Henry Clay who did a deal with Adams. Clay said he would withdraw from the election if Adams made him secretary of state. Adams agreed and, in the final vote, won a majority of two over Jackson and the remaining candidate.

ACCUSATIONS

Andrew Jackson was furious about the result and accused Henry Clay of being a Judas. The argument raged on for more than a year, and in 1826 Clay was forced to fight a duel with Senator John Randolph, who was a supporter of Jackson. Senator Randolph accused Clay of making a "corrupt bargain" with Adams. Neither was hurt. More importantly, Jackson continually accused Adams of corruption. This charge weakened Adams' government, and eventually split his **Democratic-Republican** party into two – the pro-Adams **Whigs** and Jackson's **Democrats**.

BACK TO CONGRESS

As a result of his argument with Jackson, Adams did very little in government and lost the election of 1828 to Jackson. In 1830, however, Adams won a seat in the House of Representatives. For 18 years

▲ In the election of 1824, Henry Clay withdrew after John Adams promised to make him secretary of state. Adams then went on to beat his rival, Andrew Jackson. This cartoon shows Henry Clay "silencing" Jackson by sewing up his mouth, and was meant to show how Clay did not give Jackson the chance to be president.

◀ *The Last of the Mohicans*, first published in 1826, was one of the most popular books in American literature. It tells the story of Hawkeye and his Mohican friends, Uncas and Chingachook.

he fought a long campaign against the evils of **slavery** and won much respect for his tireless efforts.

In 1848, while making yet another of his many anti-slavery speeches in **Congress**, John Quincy Adams collapsed and died, aged 80.

LIKE FATHER, LIKE SON

☆ Like his father, the second president, John Quincy Adams did not mean to be rude, but few people liked him. He was so unpopular that guests sometimes refused to come to his parties. His wife, Louisa, was a singer and harpist, but Adams was "cold, austere, and forbidding." The two are said to have argued about everything, especially the care of their children.

1828
Loses presidential election

1830
Elected to the House of Representatives

1848
Dies in Washington, D.C.

1767
Born in Waxhaw, South Carolina

1781
Fights in the Revolutionary War

1878
Becomes a lawyer

1796
Represents Tennessee in House of Representatives

1815
Defeats the British at New Orleans and becomes a major-general

1823
Elected to the Senate

1824
Loses presidential election to John Quincy Adams

▶ Jackson on horseback, fighting at the Battle of New Orleans.

When Andrew Jackson was elected president in 1828, one of his former neighbors is said to have stated: "If Andrew Jackson can become president, anyone can!" For Jackson was rough and unruly as a young man, and he liked gambling and practical jokes. However, he was also a national hero. He fought in the **Revolutionary** War and defeated the British at the Battle of New Orleans in 1815. But Jackson's path to the White House was not smooth. He led in the election of 1824 but lost to John Quincy Adams. Jackson was successful in 1828, but his opponents turned the campaign into the first **dirty election** in US history. This meant that they used information about Jackson to turn the public against him. They were able to do this because Jackson had married Rachel Robards twice – her divorce from her first husband was not finalized in time to make the first ceremony legal. Jackson's opponents accused his wife of bigamy, and she became ill as a result of the scandal. To Jackson's great sadness, she died before he became president.

☆ **TERM**
1829–1837

☆ **PARTY**
Democrat

☆ **VICE-PRESIDENTS**
*John Calhoun,
Martin Van Buren*

☆ **FIRST LADY**
None

☆ **STATES IN
THE UNION** *25*

7th president

> *The great can protect themselves, but the poor and humble require the arm and shield of the law.*
>
> **ANDREW JACKSON, 1821**

ANDREW JACKSON

▶ Jackson's assassin carried two pistols, both of which misfired, giving Jackson a chance to shoot him.

1828 Elected president

1832 Re-elected president

1835 Survives assassination attempt

1837 Retires to his estate in Tennessee

1845 Dies in Tennessee

A MAN OF FIRSTS

☆ Andrew Jackson was the only US president to kill a man in a duel (fought over his wife's honor), the only one to kill a man while in office (his would-be assassin), and the only one to be a prisoner of war (held by the British during the Revolutionary War).

BITING THE BULLET
For most of his adult life, Jackson lived with two bullets inside him. One was removed without anesthetic after 20 years; the other remained lodged near his heart until his death.

INTO OFFICE

Jackson fought the 1828 election as head of the new **Democratic Party**, which was supported by workers, farmers, and small businesses. Jackson was in favor of the "little man," and was against the political and business **establishment**. He won the election easily. At his **inauguration**, his supporters celebrated with such enthusiasm that the event almost turned into a riot.

As president, Jackson remained popular but he was not a great success. He appointed a group of his friends to help him govern, and this team was known as a "**kitchen cabinet**." These party members rewarded their own friends by giving them well-paid government jobs which led to accusations of **patronage** and corruption.

THE SURVIVOR

In 1835 an assassination attempt was made on Jackson – the first on a US president – but he survived the attack and shot the assassin dead.

Jackson also showed that he was a political survivor when he refused to get involved in the struggle fought by Texas against Mexico for its independence. Texas allowed the people that lived in the region to keep slaves. Although he kept slaves himself and supported **slavery**, Jackson did not want to upset the balance between pro- and anti-slavery states in the Union by supporting Texas.

In 1837 Jackson handed over the presidency to his **vice-president** and retired to his estate. He was as popular at the end of his political life as he had been at the beginning.

FREE TEXAS

☆ In 1835 the Mexican province of Texas revolted and declared itself an independent republic. Within a year, Texas defeated the Mexican army and elected Sam Houston as its first president. The most famous battle in the Texan war of independence was in March 1836. The Mexican army besieged the Texans in the Alamo fortress. The Texans refused to surrender and after a 12-day bombardment, the Mexicans stormed the building and killed all 187 defenders.

The final few survivors make a last stand at the Alamo

MARTIN VAN BUREN

1782
Born in Kinderhook, New York

1796
Leaves school with little formal education

1814
Elected to New York Senate

☆ **TERM**
1837–1841

☆ **PARTY**
Democrat

☆ **VICE-PRESIDENT**
Richard Johnson

☆ **FIRST LADY**
None

☆ **STATES IN THE UNION** *26*

"I cannot expect to perform the task with equal ability and success."

MARTIN VAN BUREN ON TAKING OVER FROM ANDREW JACKSON IN 1837

THE FIRST AMERICAN

Martin Van Buren was the first US president to be born an American citizen, as all his predecessors had been born British. He was also the only president who spoke Dutch as a first language.

Martin Van Buren was president for only four years. Many people believe that he did not achieve much of lasting value. Van Buren is best remembered as the man who set up a powerful organization called a "**state machine**," which helped to get his candidates elected to office. He also established the **two-party political system** that survives to this day in the US.

Van Buren was born in New York State and was the son of a farmer and innkeeper. He had little formal education and left school aged 14. Later, he learned enough law to become a lawyer. In 1814 he was elected to the New York **State Senate** and

progressed through the US Senate to become governor of his state in 1828. Van Buren then set up a political organization, known as the Albany Regency, to tighten political control over New York.

Few people were allowed to vote in those days, so it was quite easy for Martin Van Buren to make sure that they voted in the way that he wanted. Van Buren achieved control through a combination of discipline and **patronage** over voters. He used his organization to unite various groups and individuals who were opposed to John Quincy Adams as president, and he put together a winning election **campaign** for Andrew Jackson in 1828 and for himself in 1836.

When he set up the **Democratic Party**, Van Buren established the two-party system in American politics. The founding fathers who wrote the

1821
Elected to
US Senate

1828
Becomes
Governor of
New York

1829
Appointed secretary
of state under
Jackson

1832
Elected
vice-president
under Jackson

1836
Elected
president

1840
Defeated by
William Harrison

1862
Dies in
Kinderhook,
New York

◀ The *Great Western* was the first steamship to cross the Atlantic when the transatlantic service began in 1838.

Constitution thought that individual members of **Congress** would have different ideas, so there was no need to have political parties. Martin Van Buren disagreed. He believed that two-party politics was the best way to make sure that issues were debated thoroughly and that both sides of an argument were fully discussed.

This style of politics and the combination of people that formed the basis for the **Democratic Party** is still used in US politics today.

CAUTIOUS PROGRESS

As president, Van Buren was careful in everything he did. He inherited a financial crisis from Jackson, during which 618 banks went bankrupt. He solved the crisis by establishing firmer **federal** control over banks and gave the government more control over its own money. Although Van Buren was against **slavery**, he did nothing to anger the slave-owning states. He believed that slavery would end and that it would cause "terrible convulsions."

Van Buren preferred not to go to war with neighboring countries, so he worked hard to solve outstanding disputes with British-owned Canada. In 1840 he ran for president again, but he was defeated by William Harrison.

FIXING THE RESULT

☆ Van Buren was very successful at "fixing things" in politics, meaning that he was good at getting people to vote the way he thought they should. He was known as "The Little Magician" and "The Red Fox of Kinderhook," which is where he was born and lived.

Many believe that Van Buren lost this election because he refused to take over slave-owning Texas and because of a war being fought in Florida. He ran for president several times more but was never re-elected. He died in Kinderhook in 1862.

▲ During Van Buren's presidency, 18,000 members of the Cherokee Nation were removed from their homelands to the government-controlled "Indian Territory" west of the Mississippi. About 2,000 of them died on the "Trail of Tears."

25

1773
Born in Charles City County, Virginia

1791
Joins the army

1800
First governor of Indiana Territory

1811
Fights Native Americans at Tippecanoe River

1812–15
Fights British and becomes a brigadier-general

1816
Elected to House of Representatives

William Harrison earned three places in the record books. He was the second-oldest person ever to be elected president (only Ronald Reagan was older). He also had the shortest term and was the first president to die in office. At his **inauguration**, Harrison caught a cold which turned into pneumonia and killed him 31 days later.

Far more important than his record-breaking was the way that he ran his election **campaign**. The modern style of campaigning, using slogans, posters, and hand-outs, began with Harrison's campaign in 1840.

Harrison studied medicine but, at the age of 18, joined the army. For seven years he fought the Native Americans of the northwestern territories, before resigning from the army in 1798. As a result of his efforts as a soldier, he was appointed first secretary of the north-western territory. When it was split into two, he became governor of Indiana, a post that he held for 12 years. During this time, he fought many battles with the Native Americans over land, including the battle at Tippecanoe River in 1811. This battle helped to give Harrison a national reputation, as did his defeat of the British during the 1812–15 war.

☆ **TERM**
1841

☆ **PARTY**
Whig

☆ **VICE-PRESIDENT**
John Tyler

☆ **FIRST LADY**
Anna Tuthill Symmes

☆ **STATES IN THE UNION** *26*

9th president

...with a supply of cider and a pension, he would happily sit by his log cabin for the rest of his days.

A POLITICAL OPPONENT, 1840

WILLIAM HARRISON

◀ General William Harrison defeats the allied force of British and Shawnee Native Americans at the Battle of the Thames in 1813.

1825
Elected to Senate

1836
Loses presidential election to Van Buren

1840
Defeats Van Buren and is elected president

1841
Dies in Washington, D.C.

INTO POLITICS

Harrison used his military reputation to help his political career. In 1816 he was elected to the **House of Representatives**, and in 1825 he went to the **Senate**. After a brief time as **ambassador** to Colombia, he returned to politics as a leading member of the **Whig Party**. He fought and lost against Martin Van Buren in the 1836 presidential election, but returned to fight again in 1840.

THE CAMPAIGNER

This time Harrison was determined to win. With a strong campaign slogan, he traveled around the country, meeting large numbers of voters. His rival, Van Buren, did the same which turned the election into the first proper two-party struggle. It was also the first time that both candidates campaigned throughout the entire country.

While on the road, Harrison handed out campaign hats, mugs of hard cider, and model log cabins, and taught his supporters a song. The song, called *Tippecanoe and Tyler too*, referred to his victory of 1811 and to his **running mate**, John Tyler. One of its lines was "Van, Van is a used-up

man," because the Whigs thought their opponent was feeble and old, compared with their rugged hero, Harrison. The result of the election was a huge victory for Harrison, but his presidency was short-lived because he was not as rugged as he seemed. Harrison's death from pneumonia 31 days after his inauguration meant that he never had a chance to turn his ideas into action.

"LOG CABIN AND HARD CIDER"

☆ Harrison stumbled on his campaign slogan by accident. In 1840 he turned an opponent's criticism to his advantage by making "Log Cabin and Hard Cider" his campaign slogan. It appealed to people who enjoyed the simple pleasures in life. He ran his campaign from a log cabin on top of an open wagon. The voters were delighted that Harrison was handing out free mugs of hard cider, a move that made him very popular.

A book for 1841 named after Harrison's successful election slogan.

TWO MORE FIRSTS

Along with all his other presidential records, William Harrison was the only president whose grandson also became president. His wife, Anna, was the first First Lady with any formal education.

1790
Born in Charles City County, Virginia

1809
Becomes a lawyer

1811
Elected to Virginia assembly

1817
Elected to House of Representatives

1825
Becomes Governor of Virginia

1827
Elected to US Senate

▶ A former New York slave, Sojourner Truth, spoke out against slavery and for women's rights. Tyler thought each US state should make its own laws on slavery.

John Tyler did not plan to become US president. He gained the presidency when his running mate, William Harrison, died shortly after being elected. Tyler had been Harrison's **running mate** because Tyler was a southerner who helped Harrison to win much-needed votes from the southern, slave-owning states. As the first president who was not actually elected, Tyler had little support from the public, and he was often criticized for his views. His nickname of "His Accidency" stayed with him throughout his term in office. Like many US presidents, John Tyler trained as a lawyer and first entered politics in his **state assembly**. He rose through politics in Virginia to become state governor, and represented the state in both the **House of Representatives** and the **Senate**. Tyler was fiercely against **federal** control over the states and he strongly supported their right to govern themselves. Tyler was not in favor of **slavery**, but he supported the right of the southern states to make their own laws on the subject. Tyler's views resulted in quarrels with Andrew Jackson and Martin Van Buren and led him to join the opposition party of William Harrison.

☆ **TERM**
1841–1845

☆ **PARTY**
Whig

☆ **VICE-PRESIDENT**
None

☆ **FIRST LADIES**
Letitia Christian
Julia Gardiner

☆ **STATES IN THE UNION** *27*

10th president

JOHN TYLER

◀ The Lone Star was the flag of the former Texas republic. In 1844 President Tyler asked Congress to approve the takeover of Texas, which took place the following year.

◀ In 1844 Samuel Morse sent the world's first telegraph message. It was sent 40 miles, from Washington to Baltimore.

1862
Dies in Richmond, Virginia

1861
Chairs conference in Washington to avert a war

1840
Wins presidential election as running mate to Harrison

1841
Becomes president when Harrison dies

1845
Stands down as president

THE UNEXPECTED PRESIDENT

The job of president was forced on Tyler at the age of 50 and he was the youngest man up until then to become president. But Tyler was not popular.

He upset his **Whig** supporters by opposing the ideas that they supported and he failed to gain support from the **Democrats**. However, he did enjoy some successes as president. He ended a war with the **Seminole Nation** in Florida, re-organized the US Navy, reached a trade agreement with China, and encouraged settlers to move across the Mississippi to colonize the vast prairies.

BABY BOOM

☆ John Tyler had more children than any other president. His wife, Letitia Christian, had eight children before she died. Tyler then married Julia Gardiner, who was younger than three of Tyler's daughters, and they had seven more children.

Above all, Tyler began to take over the independent **republic** of Texas. But Tyler had few political friends and he decided not to fight the presidential election in 1844. Instead, he retired to his plantation in Virginia, but remained active in politics. In 1861 as a **civil war** was about to break out in the US, Tyler chaired a peace conference in Washington between the pro- and anti-slavery states. The aim of the conference was to try to avoid a war between the northern and southern states over slavery, but it was not successful. When it failed, Tyler supported the southern states that decided to leave the **Union**. He was elected to the independent **Confederate Congress** in 1861, but he died before he could take his seat.

▲ In 1841 the first wagon train of 69 pioneers crossed the Rocky Mountains on the Oregon Trail. By 1845 over 5,000 people had journeyed to the new lands of California and Oregon.

JAMES POLK

☆ **TERM**
1845–1849

☆ **PARTY**
Democrat

☆ **VICE-PRESIDENT**
George Dallas

☆ **FIRST LADY**
Sarah Childress

☆ **STATES IN THE UNION** *30*

1795
Born in Mecklenburg County, North Carolina

1818
Graduates from university and practices law

1823
Enters politics in North Carolina

> *...though I occupy a very high position, I am the hardest working man in the country*
>
> **JAMES POLK, 1845**

In 1841 James Polk's **political career looked like it was over. He was defeated in his fight to be** re-elected governor of Tennessee after two years in office, and, even worse, he was defeated again when he tried to regain the governorship in 1843. Yet, at the 1844 **Democratic Party Convention**, Polk was nominated to run for president, and went on to win the election narrowly. Polk owed his win at the Convention to the fact that his main opponent, Martin Van Buren, was opposed to bringing Texas into the **Union** because it was a pro-**slavery** state. This would upset the balance between pro- and anti-slavery states in the Union. Polk wanted to annex Texas, or add it to the Union, and was finally nominated as a candidate on the ninth **ballot**. As candidate, Polk **campaigned** on a slogan of "54–40 or fight," which referred to the latitude of the boundary line between British-run Canada and the northwestern territory of Oregon. Oregon was claimed by both Britain and the USA and, as a result, war between the two looked possible. Polk won the election and was determined to expand the Union as much as he could. In 1845 a journalist named John O'Sullivan wrote an article in which he said that it is "our manifest destiny to overspread the continent allotted by Providence for the free development of our yearly multiplying millions." Polk agreed with O'Sullivan and took charge of the biggest expansion of the US since Jefferson bought the Louisiana Territory in 1803.

Texas eventually joined the Union in 1845 as the 28th state, but Polk wanted to own the Mexican

TRUST IN NO BANK
James Polk did not trust banks and he kept all his money in bags around the house. When he died, he left all the money he had to his wife, Sarah.

1825
Elected to
House of
Representatives

1835
Speaker of
the House

1839
Elected
governor of
Tennessee

1841 & 1843
Failed to win
re-election to
governor

1844
Elected
president

1849
Steps down as
president and
soon dies

▶ From 1845–49, Ireland
suffered a terrible famine,
and up to one million Irish
people emigrated to the USA.

THE WORKAHOLIC

☆ James Polk worked hard as president. His wife, Sarah, also worked hard as his private secretary and chief adviser. Polk refused to run for a second presidential term and died, exhausted after all his efforts, three months after leaving office.

☆ James Polk was the first president to have "Hail to the Chief" played when he entered the room. He also hosted the first Thanksgiving dinner at the White House. But he banned alcohol, music, and dancing at his parties and he was said to have had no sense of humor.

provinces to its west, notably California. He made Mexico an offer of $30 million for the region, which Mexico rejected. Polk then sent General Zachary Taylor to stir things up, and war between the two countries broke out in 1846. The fight was short and one-sided. By 1848 Mexico was forced to hand over 500,000 square miles of territory in return for $18.25 million. This was known as the **Treaty** of Guadalupe-Hidalgo. The area of land included the whole of what is now California, Nevada, and Utah plus much of New Mexico, Arizona, Wyoming, and Colorado.

Meanwhile, Polk had peacefully settled the Oregon dispute with Britain by agreeing the border along the more southerly 49th latitude. The United States now reached the Pacific Ocean and now governed everything between Canada to the north and Mexico to the south.

James Polk always said that he would be president for only one term. He said at his **inauguration** that "though I occupy a very high position, I am the hardest-working man in the country." By 1849 he was exhausted and retired to his estate in Nashville, Tennessee until his death a few months later.

◀ At the battle of Resaca de la Palma, Texas, the US 2nd Dragoons fought the Mexican army four days before the official declaration of war on May 13, 1846.

ZACHARY TAYLOR

12th president

☆ **TERM**
1849–1850

☆ **PARTY**
Whig

☆ **VICE-PRESIDENT**
Millard Fillmore

☆ **FIRST LADY**
Margaret Smith

☆ **STATES IN THE UNION** *30*

OLD WARHORSE
Taylor's faithful horse, Old Whitey, came with him in retirement from the army to the White House and grazed happily on the White House lawn.

...hostilities may now be considered as commenced.

ZACHARY TAYLOR, 1846

By the mid-1840s, he was a much-admired military leader and was known as "Old Rough and Ready" for his down-to-earth approach. The war against Mexico gave Taylor his reputation as a great leader. In 1846 he advanced into Mexico on President Polk's orders. The plan was to force Mexico to declare war on the US. He achieved this aim and sent a wire to President Polk, which stated that "hostilities may now be considered as commenced," to tell him that war had started.

Taylor defeated the Mexicans at Palo Alto and Resaca de la Palma, then took their stronghold of Monterey. In 1847 he achieved his greatest victory when he defeated a force that was four times greater than his own at Buena Vista. By the time the war ended in 1848, Taylor was a national hero.

Like Andrew Jackson and William Harrison before him, Zachary Taylor became president because of his military reputation. Since Taylor's presidency was so short, he is best remembered for his military achievements.

A NATIONAL HERO

Zachary Taylor was raised in Kentucky and joined the army in 1808, aged 24. He remained in the army for 40 years, fighting the British in the war of 1812–15 and the Native Americans in many conflicts around the **Union**.

1784
Born in Orange County, Virginia

1808
Joins the US army

1810
Becomes a captain

1812
Promoted to major for his defense of Fort Harrison

1832
Becomes a colonel

1846–48
Commands army war against Mexic

32

THE GOLD RUSH

⭐ In March 1848, the first newspaper reports appeared about the discovery of gold near the American River in California. Within a year, more than 80,000 people headed west to seek their fortune in California. About 10,000 Australians crossed the Pacific Ocean, while many more prospectors arrived from Europe and South America. Some became rich, but many lost their money on gambling and other illegal activities.

Early gold prospectors try their luck

A GOOD CAMPAIGN

The **Whig Party** was keen to regain the presidency in 1848 from the **Democrats**, who had captured it from them four years earlier. In order to achieve this goal, they convinced Taylor to stand for them in the presidential election. Taylor had never even voted in a presidential election, but he ran a good **campaign** and won the election.

As president, Taylor governed a country that was increasingly divided on the problem of **slavery**. Although he was a southerner and kept slaves himself, Taylor believed that slavery should not be allowed in any new states that wanted to join the Union. However, he was happy for existing slave-owning states to keep slavery.

Before he had time to settle this sensitive issue, Taylor died in Washington in July 1850 at the age of 65. Zachary Taylor had achieved little of lasting importance during his two years as president.

◀ Zachary Taylor, dressed in uniform as an American army commander on his horse, Old Whitey. Taylor was well known across the Union for his heroics in battle, in particular during the Mexican War of 1846–48.

1848
Elected president

1850
Dies in Washington, D.C.

▲ In 1849 during Taylor's presidency, 20 people died in riots outside the Astor Place Opera House in New York City.

33

MILLARD FILLMORE

⭐ **TERM**
1850–1853

⭐ **PARTY**
Whig

⭐ **VICE-PRESIDENT**
None

⭐ **FIRST LADY**
Abigail Powers

⭐ **STATES IN THE UNION** *31*

A WORKING LADY

Millard Fillmore's wife, Abigail, was the first First Lady to have a job. She worked as a teacher and taught her future husband when he was catching up on his missed schooling at the age of 19.

Millard Fillmore **became president on the death of Zachary Taylor, but his own term in** office was also short and was totally dominated by the subject of **slavery**. He was not a strong enough president to bring a solution to this problem.

EARLY LIFE

Fillmore was born and brought up in New York. He was not well educated, although he trained as a lawyer while in his early 20s. As a member of the New York **state assembly**, he made himself popular by sponsoring a government **bill** that changed the law so that people who were in debt could not be imprisoned. In 1833 Fillmore was elected to the **House of Representatives**, where he joined the **Whigs**, and was a useful party member. He was a natural choice to become the **vice-presidential** candidate under Zachary Taylor, but he was ill-prepared to become president himself.

▶ In 1851 a US yacht raced 14 British yachts around the Isle of Wight in England and won. The yacht was called *The America* and the race is now called the America's Cup.

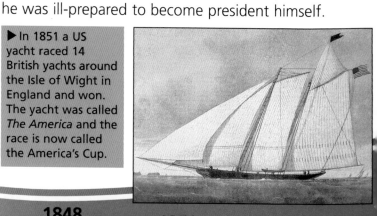

1800
Born in Cayuga County, New York

1823
Becomes a lawyer

1829
Elected to New York state assembly

1833
First elected to House of Representatives

1848
Elected vice-president under Zachary Taylor

1850
Becomes president on Taylor's death

THE COMPROMISER

As president, Fillmore had to face the problem of slavery, which was rapidly tearing the **Union** apart. Fillmore wanted to reach an agreement between the two sides and was willing to compromise in order to get it. **Congress** debated the subject for months before a series of proposals, known as the "Compromise of 1850," was eventually agreed by President Fillmore.

The Compromise allowed California to join the Union as a **free state**, let New Mexico and Utah make their own choices, and abolished slavery in the District of Columbia.

▶ President Fillmore's wife, Abigail Powers, was responsible for setting up a library in the White House.

The Compromise also included the *Fugitive Slave Act*, which made it compulsory to return runaway slaves to their original owners from anywhere in the country. President Fillmore enforced this act firmly, and he upset anti-slavery campaigners in the northern states. The Compromise did, however, make the southern states more content.

TO JAPAN

In 1852 Fillmore sent Commander Matthew Perry to Japan to force the Japanese to open up their ports to western shipping and trade. A **treaty** between the two countries was signed in 1854, opening up trade links and ending 150 years of Japanese isolation.

IN RETIREMENT

Fillmore had hoped to make the Whigs an obvious choice to run the government, as it was a compromise party between the pro- and anti-slavery forces. His party failed to re-nominate him for the presidency in 1852, however, and he stepped down as president. He fought for the presidency again as an **Independent** in 1856, but got little support and retired to Buffalo, New York, where he was active in local affairs until his death.

CLASSIC LITERATURE

☆ In 1852 the famous book called *Uncle Tom's Cabin, or, Life Among the Lowly* was published. The story, which was written by Harriet Beecher Stowe, was about an African-American slave who rescues a white child. The book sold 300,000 copies after it was published and was made into a play.

Moby-Dick, or, The Whale was published by Herman Melville in 1851. It tells the tale of Captain Ahab and his pursuit of a white whale. Although difficult to read and slow to sell, the book soon became a classic of American literature.

Sales advertisement for Stowe's classic story

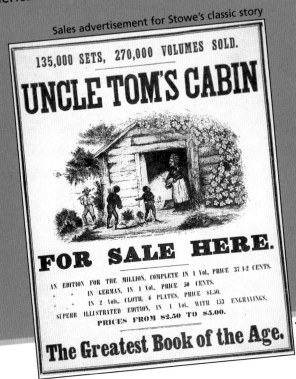

135,000 SETS, 270,000 VOLUMES SOLD.

UNCLE TOM'S CABIN
FOR SALE HERE.

AN EDITION FOR THE MILLION, COMPLETE IN 1 Vol., PRICE 37 1-2 CENTS.
" " IN GERMAN, IN 1 Vol., PRICE 50 CENTS.
" " IN 2 Vols., CLOTH, 6 PLATES, PRICE $1.50.
SUPERB ILLUSTRATED EDITION, IN 1 Vol., WITH 153 ENGRAVINGS,
PRICES FROM $2.50 TO $5.00.

The Greatest Book of the Age.

1850
Agrees to slavery compromise

1852
Fails to be re-nominated for president by his Whig Party

1856
Runs for president again

1874
Dies in Buffalo, New York

1804
Born in Hillsboro,
New Hampshire

1827
Becomes
a lawyer

1829
Enters politics in
New Hampshire

1833
Elected to House
of Representatives

1837
Elected to
the Senate

▶ In 1853 Commander Perry met
some representatives of the Japanese
emperor in Japan. A treaty between
the two countries was signed in 1854.

In 1852 half the states in the Union were against slavery and the other half were for slavery. As this subject continued to divide the northern from the southern states, the US needed a strong president. Instead, the people elected Franklin Pierce, who was a compromise candidate – a man who only won his party's nomination on the 49th **ballot**.

THE COMPROMISE

Franklin Pierce made his reputation as a politician in New Hampshire. He was also an effective member of both the **House of Representatives** and the **Senate**. In addition, he fought in the Mexican War. Although he represented a northern state – New Hampshire – he actually supported the slave owners of the South. In theory, that made him an ideal candidate to unite both his own party and the country, and he won the presidential election in 1852 by a **landslide** against his **Whig** opponent.

KANSAS AND NEBRASKA

Once in office, Pierce supported the slave owners and failed to stop the rising opposition to **slavery**. He also failed to unite his country. In 1854 he approved the *Kansas-Nebraska Act*, which overturned the **Missouri Compromise** of 1820. The Act allowed the territories in the northern part of the old **Louisiana Purchase** to choose whether or not to allow slavery. Until then, they had not been allowed to

☆ **TERM**
1853–1857

☆ **PARTY**
Democrat

☆ **VICE-PRESIDENT**
William King

☆ **FIRST LADY**
Jane Appleton

☆ **STATES IN THE UNION** *31*

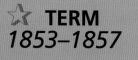

14th president

FRANKLIN PIERCE

HOME COMFORTS
Pierce and his wife did much to modernize the White House, installing central heating and a second bathroom. Pierce was also the first president to have a Christmas tree in the White House.

► In the poem, *The Song of Hiawatha*, written in 1855, Henry Longfellow tells the tale of a Native American and his love, Minnehaha.

► In 1853 Levi Strauss began to sell heavyweight cotton trousers to miners in California. These were the first blue jeans.

1846–48
Fights in Mexican War

1852
Wins presidential election

1854
Approves Kansas-Nebraska Act

1856
Fails to win re-nomination as Democratic presidential candidate

1869
Dies in Concord, New Hampshire

make this decision. A local war almost started in Kansas, and riots broke out in Boston and in other cities that were against the Act. Many people threatened to disobey the *Fugitive Slave Act* and not return runaway slaves to their owners.

ONE SUCCESS

In 1853 Pierce had a great success when he negotiated the **Gadsden Purchase** from Mexico for $10 million. This added to the US 29,460 square miles of Mexican territory west of New Mexico. The land was bought so that the important southern railroad to California would be able to pass entirely through US territory.

Pierce planned to take over Cuba (owned by Spain) if the slave revolt there spread to the southern US states. This upset many people and other mistakes almost caused a war with both Spain and Britain. As a result, Pierce's own party did not re-nominate him for president, and he retired. He died in 1869, after the **Civil War** that he had not been able to prevent.

► Throughout the southern states, African-Americans were forced to work as slaves on cotton and fruit plantations.

THE REPUBLICAN PARTY

☆ In 1854 a group of Democrats and Whigs that were against slavery met in Ripon, Wisconsin. They agreed that if the *Kansas-Nebraska Act* became law, they would form a new party to fight against slavery. The Act did become law, and the new party was formed. It was called the Republican Party. The party held its first state Convention in Jackson, Michigan, in July 1854 and fought its first presidential election in 1856. The group chose the name "Republican" in honor of Thomas Jefferson, the first Democratic-Republican president, who was an opponent of slavery, even though he kept slaves himself.

JAMES BUCHANAN

15th president

★ **TERM**
1857–1861

★ **PARTY**
Democrat

★ **VICE-PRESIDENT**
John Breckinridge

★ **FIRST LADY**
None

★ **STATES IN
THE UNION** *33*

1791	1821	1832	1834
Born near Mercersburg, Pennsylvania	Elected to House of Representatives	Becomes ambassador to Russia	Elected to Senate

> *If you are as happy on entering this house as I am at leaving it… you are the happiest man in this country.*

**JAMES BUCHANAN TO
ABRAHAM LINCOLN, 1861**

When he was elected president in 1856, James Buchanan was **probably the wrong person to lead his** country. He was a pro-**slavery Democrat** who favored the southern states, but his policies failed to keep his country together.

Buchanan had trained as a lawyer and made his reputation in the **House of Representatives** and the **Senate**. He also served as **ambassador** to Russia and then Britain. While in Britain in 1854, he drafted what was known as the Ostend Manifesto with the US ambassadors to France and Spain.

A slave revolt in Spanish-owned Cuba had threatened to spread to the southern states of America. Buchanan had suggested that if Spain would not sell Cuba to the US, the island should be seized by force. Cuba would then became a slave-owning state in the **Union**. The secret Ostend Manifesto that was drafted to secure this deal soon became public and it caused an outcry among anti-slavery campaigners.

Although the government rejected the manifesto, Buchanan gained great popularity in the southern states for his views. As a result, he won the Democratic nomination for presidency.

A NATION DIVIDED

As president, Buchanan governed a country that was split between pro- and anti-slavery states. Buchanan believed that the **federal** government had no right to tell the slave states what laws they should live by. He thought that territories joining the Union should decide for themselves whether to allow slavery or not.

1845
Secretary of
state under
President Polk

1853
Ambassador
to Britain

1856
Wins
presidential
election for
Democrats

1859
John Brown
is hanged in
Virginia

1861
Steps down
as president

1868
Dies in
Lancaster,
Pennsylvania

▶ The first oil well in the world was drilled in Pennsylvania, by Edwin Drake in 1859.

▲ In 1860 the first Pony Express carried mail from Missouri to California.

In 1857 in a case known as the Dred Scott case, the **Supreme Court** ruled that slaves and their descendants were property, not people. In addition, the Court ruled that the **Missouri Compromise** of 1820 was unconstitutional, or against the rules in the **Constitution**. This was because the Constitution gave rights to all states to keep slaves, whereas the Compromise did not allow slavery in the northern part of the **Louisiana Purchase**.

Buchanan made things worse by approving a pro-slavery constitution for Kansas. He also harshly enforced the *Fugitive Slave Act*. By 1859 the country was in turmoil.

JOHN BROWN'S BODY

In October 1859 John Brown and a group of militant **abolitionists** seized an arsenal, or a supply of weapons, at Harper's Ferry in Virginia. They planned to use the weapons to help slaves win their freedom by fighting against their owners. John Brown was captured and hanged in December 1859. His actions caused fears in the South that abolitionists in the North wanted to bring about an uprising by the slaves in their states.

▲ On December 2, 1859, the anti-slavery campaigner, John Brown, was led out of his prison cell in Charleston, West Virginia, and taken to the gallows where he was hanged.

A DIVIDED COUNTRY

In 1860 the two parties chose their candidates for the forthcoming presidential election. The new **Republican Party** chose Abraham Lincoln who was against slavery. The Democrats were divided, and they chose two opposing candidates – the pro-slavery, current **vice-president**, John Breckinridge, and **Senator** Stephen Douglas who believed that states should choose for themselves whether to keep slaves or not.

Lincoln won, and the country finally split into two. The **Civil War** was about to begin.

THE SINGLE PRESIDENT

⭐ James Buchanan never married, so his niece, Harriet Lane, was hostess at his White House parties. People thought Buchanan might be lonely in the White House, so they sent him pets for company, including a pair of bald eagles and a Newfoundland dog.

1809
Born in
Hardin,
Kentucky

1831
Moves to
Illinois

1834–42
Member of the
Illinois state
legislature

1846
Elected to
House of
Representatives

1856
Joins
Republican
Party

1858
Challenges
Stephen
Douglas to
debates

1860
Elected
president

◄ The log cabin where President Lincoln was
born in 1809 and lived for seven years.

At the most difficult time in its history, the United States of America elected as president a man who came from a poor family and had little formal schooling and only two years' experience in national politics. Yet Abraham Lincoln did the job well, and many people believe that he is the finest president that the US has ever had.

FROM A LOG CABIN TO THE LAW

Lincoln was born in a log cabin in Kentucky. His family moved to Indiana where Lincoln educated himself, reading the Bible, Shakespeare, and many other books. In 1831 he moved to Illinois and trained as a lawyer, setting up a legal practice in 1837. He was elected to the state **legislature**, but he did not make much of the job. After eight years, he returned to work in the law.

ANTI-SLAVERY POLITICS

In 1846 Lincoln was elected to the **House of Representatives**. He was not a great success and retired to Illinois in 1849. He entered national politics for the second time in 1854 when the Illinois **senator**, Stephen Douglas, put the *Kansas-Nebraska Act* through **Congress**. This Act legalized **slavery**. Lincoln was against slavery and

☆ **TERM**
1861–1865

☆ **PARTY**
Republican

☆ **VICE-PRESIDENTS**
*Hannibal Hamlin,
Andrew Johnson*

☆ **FIRST LADY**
Mary Todd

☆ **STATES IN
THE UNION** *36*

16th president

...this nation, under God, shall have a new birth of freedom.

**FROM LINCOLN'S
GETTYSBURG ADDRESS,
NOVEMBER 19, 1863**

ABRAHAM LINCOLN

▶ Lincoln's famous address, in Gettysburg in 1863, lasted only a few minutes.

▶ Lincoln is shot in a Washington theatre by John Wilkes Booth.

1865
Assassinated in
Ford's Theatre,
Washington

1861
Civil War
breaks out

1863
Signs Emancipation
Proclamation to
free slaves

1863
Delivers
Gettysburg
address

1864
Re-elected
president

did not want it to spread to the western territories. He joined the new, anti-slavery **Republican Party** and, in a series of debates, he challenged Douglas for his **Senate** seat. "I believe this government cannot endure permanently half-slave and half-free," he said. Lincoln won the debates, but he lost the election. By now, he was a national figure, and, in 1860, he stood as the Republican candidate for president. When he won, 11 southern states left the **Union** and the **Civil War** broke out.

FREEING THE SLAVES

Lincoln wanted to keep the Union together, and, at first, he did nothing about slavery. His government was split between **abolitionists** and those who

DEATH THREATS

☆ As president, Lincoln received more than 10,000 death threats. He kept some of them in his desk at the White House, in an envelope marked "Assassinations." In response to these threats, he said: "I cannot bring myself to believe that any human being lives who would do me any harm."

thought the **Confederates** would win. Lincoln did not take either side at first, but, after several victories, he signed the Emancipation Proclamation, which set all slaves free. In reality, the proclamation meant nothing. He did not have the constitutional authority to abolish slavery and he did not have any power over the **Confederacy**. But the proclamation turned the war from a fight against **secession** into a crusade to abolish slavery.

VICTORY AND DEATH

Lincoln did not want a war. At his Gettysburg address, he dedicated a cemetery to those who had died in battle. His speech proclaimed "a new birth of freedom" in the US. Lincoln did not live to see that freedom. One week after the surrender of the Confederates in 1865, Lincoln was assassinated in Washington by a southern fanatic, John Wilkes Booth.

THE CIVIL WAR

☆ When Abraham Lincoln became president in 1861, South Carolina and ten pro-slavery southern states left the Union and formed the Confederacy. On April 12, Confederate forces attacked the Union forces at Fort Sumter, and war broke out. The Confederates were led by Robert E. Lee and "Stonewall" Jackson. At first they won most of the battles, but by 1864 the Union forces under General Ulysses Grant took control and won the four-year war in 1865.

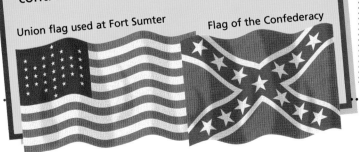

Union flag used at Fort Sumter   Flag of the Confederacy

▶ The 54th Massachusetts, the first Black regiment after Emancipation, storming Fort Wagner in 1863.

ANDREW JOHNSON

⭐ **TERM**
1865–1869

⭐ **PARTY**
Democrat

⭐ **VICE-PRESIDENT**
None

⭐ **FIRST LADY**
Eliza McCardle

⭐ **STATES IN THE UNION** *37*

"His faith in people never wavered."

EPITAPH ON HIS GRAVESTONE

SEWN UP
Throughout his life Andrew Johnson made his own suits, and was skilled at needlework and making quilts.

The Civil War made, and also destroyed, Andrew Johnson. He was the only southern state **senator** to remain loyal to the **Union**, and became a hero to those who were struggling to keep the country united during the **Civil War**. Yet after the war, Johnson failed to lead the country to a peaceful future.

TAILORED FOR OFFICE

Andrew Johnson was born into a poor family and, at 14, he was apprenticed to a tailor. He soon set up his own tailor's shop and, with his wife's help, became well educated. He was taught to write and spell by his wife, Eliza, whom he married when he was aged 19. She was 16 years old. In 1828 Johnson became alderman of Greenville and then mayor, starting a public career in the **Democratic Party** that was to last for more than 40 years. Johnson was a skilled debater but, unusually for a southerner, he was opposed to the slave owners and did not wish to extend **slavery** to the new territories in the west.

HIS FINEST HOUR

Johnson's finest hour came in 1861. As senator for the state of Tennessee, he was expected to join the **Confederacy** when Civil War broke out. But Johnson was a strong supporter of the Union, and he was the only southerner who remained in the US **Senate**. As a reward, Johnson was appointed military governor of Tennessee. Before the end of the war, he was able to set up a new local government in Tennessee, which had been run by the army.

1808
Born in Raleigh, North Carolina

1835
Enters politics in Tennessee

1843
Elected to House of Representatives

1853
Governor of Tennessee

1857
Elected to Senate

1861
Remains in Senate after Tennessee joins Confederacy

1864
Elected vice-president to Lincoln

1865
Becomes president on Lincoln's death

FIRST IMPEACHMENT

⭐ In 1868 Andrew Johnson was the first, and until Bill Clinton the only, president to face impeachment by Congress, which means they tried to remove him from office. He was charged with "high crimes and misdemeanors." The Senate was one vote short of the number it needed to convict him, so Johnson remained in office.

Ticket to Johnson's impeachment

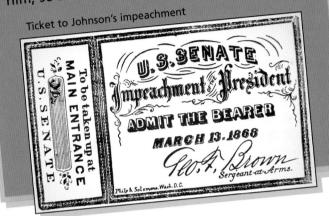

In 1864 Abraham Lincoln made Johnson his **running mate** in the presidential election. This provided a balance between a northern **Republican** president and a southern Democrat **vice-president**.

On the assassination of President Lincoln, Johnson became president. He faced an impossible task of fixing the many problems left by the war.

Politically, Johnson had few friends. The South and the Democrats thought he was a traitor and the North and the Republicans distrusted him for his southern ideals. Both sides thought he was too rigid in his views and not clever enough to run the country at such a time. Only a man like Lincoln could have coped with all the problems – and Johnson was not such a strong president.

A CLASH OF VIEWS

As president, Johnson faced an angry **Congress**. It overruled him on many occasions and passed the *Tenure of Office Act* to prevent him dismissing officials that were approved by Congress. In 1867 events came to a head when the secretary of war, Edwin Stanton, told him that the military governors in charge of the southern states were answerable to Congress and not to the president. Johnson fired Stanton, breaking the *Tenure of Office Act*. This led to his **impeachment** before Congress. He just managed to keep his job.

NORTHERN SUCCESS

The main success of Johnson's term of office came in 1867 when he bought the vast northern territory of Alaska from Russia for $7 million. But this was a minor triumph, and Johnson did not seek re-election as president. Instead, he retired to Tennessee. Although Johnson returned to the Senate in 1875, his political life was over and he died soon after taking his Senate post.

RECONSTRUCTION

⭐ After the Civil War ended, Johnson and Congress began to rebuild and reform the southern states in a program known as "Reconstruction." This slowly restored civilian government to the states and allowed them to rejoin the Union. In 1868 the 14th Amendment to the Constitution became law. It granted full citizenship to former slaves. However, many southern states continued to deny African-American people the right to vote or sit in the state governments.

1868
Senate fails to impeach him

1869
Steps down as president

◀ Cartoonists joked that Johnson would have to ask polar bears to vote for him in the empty state of Alaska.

◀ In 1868 the Sioux signed a peace treaty.

1875
Returns to the Senate

1875
Dies in Carter's Station, Tennessee

ULYSSES GRANT

★ **TERM**
1869–1877

★ **PARTY**
Republican

★ **VICE-PRESIDENTS**
Schuyler Colfax;
Henry Wilson

★ **FIRST LADY**
Julia Dent

★ **STATES IN**
THE UNION *38*

Let us have peace.

PRESIDENTIAL ACCEPTANCE
SPEECH, 1868

NEW NAME GRANT

Grant was originally named Hiram Ulysses Grant, but at West Point he discovered that he had been registered as Ulysses Simpson Grant. He kept his new name for the rest of his life.

Ulysses S. Grant was the man who won the Civil War for the Union. He was rewarded by being elected president twice. Although he remained popular throughout his eight years, Grant had his problems as president. In fact, his government was often rocked by scandal.

CONSTANT FAILURE

Grant was the son of a leather tanner. He was not especially talented as a child and when he graduated from the famous West Point Military Academy his only real skill was horse riding. In 1843 Grant entered the army and fought in the Mexican War of 1846–48. He eventually resigned in disgrace in 1854 after he was posted to the West Coast and began drinking too much because he was missing his wife. Grant then went to work for his father, and his military career seemed to be over.

In 1861 Grant rejoined the army to fight for the **Union** in the **Civil War**. He discovered that he had a natural ability to lead a large army that was fighting a difficult war.

▶ In 1870 Louisa Swain became the first American woman to vote in an election when women won that right in Wyoming.

1822
Born in Point
Pleasant, Ohio

1843
Graduates from
West Point
Military Academy

1854
Forced to resign
from the army for
excessive drinking

1861
Rejoins army
at start of
Civil War

1864
Takes
command of
Union forces

1868
Wins
presidency for
Republicans

▲ On May 10, 1869, the Union Pacific and Central Pacific railroads met at Promontory Point, Utah. The railroad now linked together the east and west coasts of America for the first time. A golden spike was hammered into the railroad to celebrate the historic occasion.

In the western territories, the settlers and the Native Americans were having a bitter struggle over who owned the land. The growth of industry in the big cities was changing the economy in the North dramatically, and this also caused many problems.

Grant was not experienced in politics and he did not cope well with these challenges. He appointed to the **Cabinet** his friends and supporters who soon took bribes. Although Grant was an honest man, the members of his government were not, and they were attacked from all sides.

IN RETIREMENT

In 1876 the Republicans chose another candidate for president, and Grant retired. He went on a successful world tour, but on his return he invested money in a corrupt bank which went out of business. Grant was bankrupt and dying of cancer, so he hurriedly wrote a book about his life to provide for his wife and family. The book was published a few days before his death and it was a huge success. This proved that, despite his mistakes as president, Grant was a much-loved figure whose military career had saved the Union from collapse.

He captured the **Confederate** Fort Donelson in 1862 and told its commander that "no terms except immediate and unconditional surrender can be accepted." He earned the nickname "Unconditional Surrender" Grant and, by 1864, he was in charge of all the Union forces. On April 9, 1865, the Confederate forces led by General Robert Lee surrendered to Grant at Appomattox Courthouse, Virginia.

PRESIDENTIAL SCANDAL

Grant was a hero of the Union. The **Republicans** chose him to fight for the 1868 election, which he won easily. The country needed a strong, firm leader because it was going through many changes.

In the South, **Reconstruction** made life even more difficult than it was before for the Black community.

SILENTLY SQUEAMISH

☆ Although he spent much of his life in the army and in battle, Grant hated the sight of blood and as a child refused to work in his father's tannery.

☆ As president, Grant was a man of few words. For one speech, he just said, "Gentlemen, in response it will be impossible to do more than thank you," and sat down.

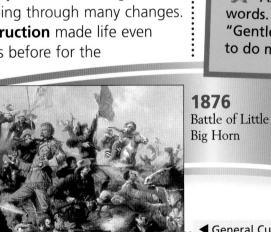

1870
American women vote for the first time

1872
Re-elected as president

1876
Battle of Little Big Horn

1877
Steps down as president

1877–79
Tours the world

1880
Fails to gain nomination for presidency

1885
Dies near Saratoga, New York

◀ General Custer and 265 US troops were killed at Little Big Horn, Dakota, by 25,500 Sioux and Cheyenne Native Americans in June 1876.

Rutherford Hayes became a national figure as governor of Ohio, **where he proved that he was an able and** competent administrator and reformer. He was honest but dull, yet the way he ran the country was controversial from the first day.

THE END OF RECONSTRUCTION

Hayes became president in the most extraordinary circumstances. Although he was runner-up in both popular and **Electoral College** votes, he won by promising to withdraw troops from the occupied southern states, which ended **Reconstruction**.

The opposition **Democrats** were outraged and called him "His Fraudulency" and called his election "The Great Swap." Hayes carried out his promise and withdrew the remaining troops from Louisiana and South Carolina. Many people in the southern states resented those in the North after their defeat in the **Civil War**. Hayes wanted to make sure that the southern states were welcomed back into the **Union**. But his attitude to the South angered the **Republican Party**, because the Republicans were in favor of harsh penalties against the southern states.

NO. 1
Hayes was the first president to use the telephone, which was invented by Alexander Graham Bell in 1876. His phone number in the White House was '1'.

AGAINST CORRUPTION

After the corruption of Ulysses Grant's presidency, Hayes tried to make the government more honest. He stopped the system of appointing friends and party supporters to senior positions. Instead, he introduced a system that was based on ability and not on "who you know." This policy was attacked by both parties, which had

He serves his party best who serves his country best.

RUTHERFORD HAYES,
1877

☆ **TERM**
1877–1881

☆ **PARTY**
Republican

☆ **VICE-PRESIDENT**
William Wheeler

☆ **FIRST LADY**
Lucy Webb

☆ **STATES IN THE UNION** *38*

19th president

RUTHERFORD HAYES

1822
Born in Delaware, Ohio

1845
Graduates from Harvard Law School

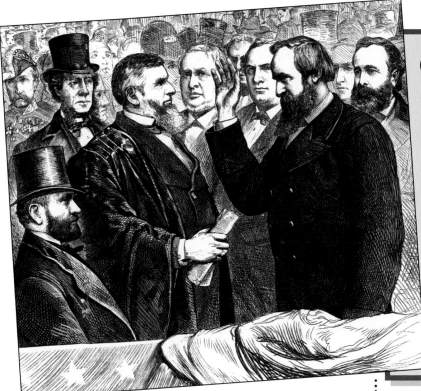

⭐ In the election of 1876, the Democrat Samuel Tilden won 4,287,670 votes, and Hayes won 4,035,924. Tilden beat Hayes by 184 to 165 in the Electoral College, which was one short of the total needed for victory. Twenty Electoral College votes from three southern states were disputed. The contested election was decided by a special committee of Congress. Hayes promised to remove troops from the occupied southern states. As a result, the committee divided along party lines and the Republican majority gave all 20 votes to Hayes, who won the election by one vote.

▲ Hayes was an honest president, but his presidency was controversial from the day that he was sworn into office in 1877. His opponents thought that he had won the election by fraud and were against him during his years in office.

always made sure that their own supporters were given the best government jobs. Hayes was not completely successful in getting rid of corruption. He did, however, have great success in firing the powerful New York customs collector, the future president, Chester Arthur. He was also successful in improving the nation's finances and providing schooling for African-American pupils.

ONE-TERM HAYES

Hayes was made more unpopular as president because his wife never drank alcohol. She was nicknamed "Lemonade Lucy" because she did not serve alcohol in the White House. Hayes always said that he would only be president for one term and, in 1881, he stepped down from office. He returned to Ohio and devoted himself to charitable work until his death.

▶ Lucy Hayes was the first First Lady to have gone to college. She supported equal rights for women, though she thought that women should not vote.

▶ In 1879 Thomas Edison patented the lightbulb.

1861
Enlists in army during Civil War

1865
Elected to House of Representatives

1867–1877
Governor of Ohio

1876
Wins presidential election for Republicans

1877
Ends Reconstruction

1881
Leaves office to do charitable work in Ohio

1893
Dies in Fremont, Ohio

JAMES GARFIELD

☆ **TERM**
1881

☆ **PARTY**
Republican

☆ **VICE-PRESIDENT**
Chester Arthur

☆ **FIRST LADY**
Lucretia Rudolph

☆ **STATES IN THE UNION** *38*

1831
Born in Cuyahoga County, Ohio

1856
Teaches ancient languages and literature

1859
Enters politics in Ohio

My God, what is there in this place that a man should ever want to get in it?

**JAMES GARFIELD
ABOUT THE
WHITE HOUSE, 1881**

James Garfield was only the second president, after Abraham Lincoln, to be assassinated while in office. He was president for less than a year, so he had little chance to leave a mark on the country. Yet James Garfield's life was full of adventure and controversy.

FROM RAGS TO WASHINGTON

James Garfield was born into a poor family on a frontier farm in the state of Ohio. As a youth, he worked as a farmer, canal boatman, and carpenter. He graduated from Williams College in 1856.

In Hiram, Ohio, Garfield was a teacher of ancient languages and literature at the Western Reserve Eclectic Institute, which was later renamed the Hiram Institute. He soon became the principal of the college, while at the same time training as a minister of the church and as a lawyer. In 1859 he was elected to the Ohio **State Senate** as an anti-**slavery** candidate. When war broke out in 1861, Garfield joined the **Union** army, rising to become a major-general of volunteers. He left the army in 1863 when he was elected to the **House of Representatives**.

James Garfield was a strong supporter of the **Republican Party** and he enforced **Reconstruction** in the defeated southern states of the Union. Garfield also opposed President Hayes' campaign to wipe out corruption and **patronage** in the **civil service**. By 1880 Garfield was an important figure in national politics.

What happened next surprised the nation. Garfield went to the Republican Party **Convention** as a **campaign** manager for **Senator** John Sherman.

1861
Enlists in the
Union army

1863
Elected to House
of Representatives

1880
Wins presidential
election for the
Republicans

1881
Shot by
Charles
Guiteau

1881
Dies in Elberon,
New Jersey

▶ In a gunfight at the OK Corral in Tombstone, Arizona, in 1881, Deputy Marshall Wyatt Earp and his brothers, Virgil and Morgan, gunned down their rivals, the Clanton brothers.

The Convention could not decide which candidate to choose. The Convention was split between the "Stalwarts," who were supporters of the former president Ulysses Grant, and the supporters of Congressman James Blaine. Garfield worked hard to stop both candidates from winning the nomination and, after 35 **ballots**, the Convention decided to seek a compromise.

On the 36th ballot, Garfield was chosen as candidate. He was a new candidate and was known to only a few electors. With a majority of just 9,464 votes, he was elected president, defeating the **Democratic** candidate Winfield Hancock, who was a Union war hero.

SHORT TERM

When Garfield became president, his **vice-president** was Chester Arthur, a member of the Stalwarts, while James Blaine became **secretary of state**. In office, Garfield overturned the anti-corruption crusade of former president Rutherford Hayes and used patronage to reward his friends and supporters.

But many people were still upset by the way that Garfield had become president

TWO-TONGUED
James Garfield was the first president to campaign in both English and Spanish. He was also the first left-handed president.

and, on July 2, 1881, he was shot by Charles Guiteau, a Stalwart who wanted Chester Arthur to become president instead.

Garfield survived for 11 weeks before he died on September 19. The Stalwarts had won, and Arthur took over as president.

FRANK LESLIE'S ILLUSTRATED NEWSPAPER

No. 1,316.—Vol. LII

NEW YORK, JULY 16, 1881.

(Price 10 Cents.)

▶ Frank Leslie's Illustrated Newspaper, published in July 1881, shows Garfield after he has been shot by his assassin, Charles Guiteau.

1829
Born in Fairfield, Vermont

1854
Becomes a lawyer in New York

1861
Quartermaster General of New York State

1865
Builds up Republican state machine in New York

1871
Customs collector of New York

1878
Removed as customs collector by President Hayes

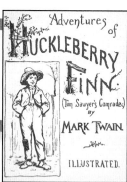

▶ Mark Twain's most famous book, *The Adventures of Huckleberry Finn*, was first published in 1884.

Throughout the presidencies of Grant, Hayes, and Garfield, the topics of patronage and corruption filled US politics. One man summed up this problem perfectly – Chester Arthur.

Arthur, the son of Irish immigrants in Vermont, studied law. When the **Republican Party** was formed in 1854, he joined immediately and soon became a major figure in New York politics. During the **Civil War**, he became Quartermaster General for New York State. His job was to make sure that essential war supplies were ready for use. Arthur was a hard worker and got on well with people. He used the contacts that he made to help the New York **Senator** Roscoe Conkling build a powerful **state machine**. In return, he was made customs collector of New York, which was the busiest and richest port in the country.

CORRUPT POLITICS

Arthur used this post to make both himself and his friends richer. The **patronage** system worked by making sure that your political friends and supporters were given well-

☆ **TERM**
1881–1885

☆ **PARTY**
Republican

☆ **VICE-PRESIDENT**
None

☆ **FIRST LADY**
None

☆ **STATES IN THE UNION** *38*

21st president

"...to gobble all the vacancies for his particular friends, and to talk reform at every gobble."

AN OBSERVER ON ARTHUR'S USE OF PATRONAGE

CHESTER ARTHUR

◀ When the Brooklyn Bridge opened in 1883, many people described it as the "Eighth Wonder of the World."

1880
Vice-president to James Garfield

1881
Becomes president on Garfield's death

1885
Steps down as president

1886
Dies in New York City

THE DANDY PRESIDENT
Arthur was nicknamed "Elegant Arthur" because he wore smart clothes and took care over his appearance.

paid and influential jobs in government, which they could use to help you to advance your own political career. Sometimes money changed hands, but more often it was influence that counted. A group of people known as "Conkling's Stalwarts," or supporters, was the biggest, most influential and most corrupt organization in Republican politics, and Chester Arthur was at the heart of it.

INTO THE PRESIDENCY

In 1880 the Republicans chose James Garfield as their presidential candidate. The Stalwarts had wanted the former president Ulysses S. Grant to be candidate but when he lost, they had to settle for Chester Arthur as **vice-presidential** candidate instead. After Garfield was murdered in 1881, Arthur became president. Many were horrified at the prospect, as they feared that Arthur would fill the government with his supporters.

To everyone's surprise, Arthur turned his back on his corrupt ways.

He pledged to get rid of patronage, and did nothing to help his former Stalwart friends. In 1883 he signed the *Pendleton Civil Service Reform Act*, which set up a **civil service** based on ability and merit, not on party patronage. Arthur also reformed the post office and other organizations.

As a result, Arthur lost the support of the Stalwarts, and the Republican Party was seriously weakened. In 1884 the Party chose his old rival, James Blaine, as their presidential candidate. Arthur became fatally ill and stepped down as president in 1885. He died the following year.

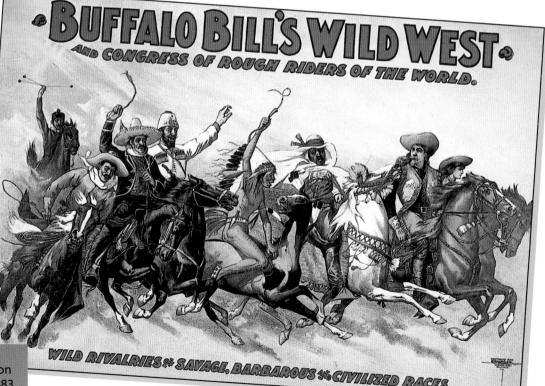

▶ William Frederick Cody, who was nicknamed "Buffalo Bill," first put on his successful *Wild West Show* in 1883.

GROVER CLEVELAND

22nd & 24th president

☆ **TERMS**
1885–1889
1893–1897

☆ **PARTY**
Democrat

☆ **VICE-PRESIDENTS**
Thomas Hendricks,
Adlai Stevenson

☆ **FIRST LADY**
Frances Folsom

☆ **STATES IN THE UNION** *38, 45*

> *A public office is a public trust.*
> **CAMPAIGN SLOGAN, 1884**

WHITE HOUSE WEDDING
Grover Cleveland was the only president to marry while in the White House. His wife, Frances, was 27 years younger than him.

Grover Cleveland is the **only president in the history of the United States of America to have served** two separate terms as president. In the first term, he was successful, but it may have been better if he had not returned for a second term.

MR. CLEAN
Grover Cleveland was the son of a Presbyterian member of the clergy. He studied law and began to practice in Buffalo, New York. He was hardworking, efficient, and honest, and having these qualities worked to his advantage as a politician. He joined the **Democratic Party** and, in 1881, made his reputation as mayor of Buffalo. While he was mayor, he stopped the corruption and **patronage** in the city hall. From there, his rise in politics was fast.

The next year, he became a successful governor of New York, and continued to fight corruption. In 1884 he was chosen as the presidential candidate for the Democratic Party. His **Republican** opponent, James Blaine, was linked to corruption. Cleveland was untainted by corruption, so he became the first Democratic president to be elected since before the **Civil War**.

1837
Born in Caldwell, New Jersey

1859
Becomes a lawyer in Buffalo, New York

1881
Anti-corruption mayor of Buffalo

1882
Governor of New York State

1884
Elected president

1888
Loses to Benjamin Harrison

1892
Regains presidency for second time

1893
Economic slump causes widespread unemployment

MAKING CHANGES

As president, Grover Cleveland continued President Chester Arthur's policy of **reforming** the **civil service**, but Cleveland was sensible enough to keep those Republicans who were good at their jobs. High **tariffs** had been in place since the Civil War in order to raise money for the government. Cleveland lost support from many in his own party when he tried to remove these tariffs. People in business liked the tariffs because they made them richer, but the ordinary working people disliked the tariffs because they caused high prices for many goods. In the 1888 presidential election, Grover Cleveland was opposed by the Republican Benjamin Harrison, who favored keeping the tariffs in place. Cleveland won the majority of the popular vote, but he lost the election in the **Electoral College**.

NOT SO POPULAR

Harrison was an unpopular and inefficient president and, in 1892, Cleveland swept back into power. But his second term in office was not successful.

The economy was in a state of disorder, and many workers were losing their jobs. Violent fights broke out between business owners and workers.

Many of the workers were now organized in **trade unions**. The government sent in **federal** troops to get the US mail on the move when it was held up because of a rail strike. Many workers were angered by this action and by the other tough measures that were taken by Cleveland.

In 1896 the Democratic Party was divided on the subject of how to deal with the **economic depression**, or the slump in the US economy, and Cleveland was not re-nominated for president. It was the end of his political life.

THE STATUE OF LIBERTY

⭐ The world-famous Statue of Liberty was designed by the French sculptor Frédéric-Auguste Bartholdi. It was built as a monument to freedom. The statue towers 305ft (93m) above the ground and stands on an island in New York City's harbor. The statue was unveiled by President Cleveland on October 28, 1886.

The Statue of Liberty

▲ The American Bison was almost extinct by 1893. This picture, *The Last of the Buffalo*, was painted by Albert Bierstadt in 1888 and helped to save them from extinction.

1897
Steps down from presidency

1908
Dies in Princeton, New Jersey

BENJAMIN HARRISON

☆ **TERM**
1889–1893

☆ **PARTY**
Republican

☆ **VICE-PRESIDENT**
Levi Morton

☆ **FIRST LADY**
Caroline Scott

☆ **STATES IN THE UNION** *44*

Grandfather's Hat Fits Ben

CAMPAIGN SLOGAN, 1888

SHOCKING BEHAVIOR
Harrison installed electric lights in the White House but was so scared of electric shocks that he left them on all the time.

Benjamin Harrison is the only president whose grandfather – William Harrison – was also president. Harrison's great-grandfather, who was also called Benjamin, had signed the **Declaration of Independence**, while his father served in the **Senate**. Politics was in the younger Benjamin Harrison's blood, but when he finally reached the presidency, he achieved very little.

As a young man, Harrison trained as a lawyer in Cincinnati before moving to Indianapolis in 1854. For the next 26 years he practiced business law and only stopped for a while during the **Civil War**, when he led a regiment of volunteers that he had organized himself. Harrison was active in **Republican** politics, but he failed twice to win the governorship of Indiana. In 1880 he won election to the US **Senate** but was defeated in 1886. His political life looked to be over.

INTO THE WHITE HOUSE

In 1888 Harrison attended the Republican Party **Convention** and surprisingly he was elected presidential candidate. He won the election against Grover Cleveland because Harrison said he would keep the **tariffs** on imported goods as high as possible. His election marked the

1833
Born in North Bend, Ohio

1852
Graduates from Miami University, Ohio

1854
Moves to Indianapolis and practices law

1861
Commands Indiana volunteer regiment in Civil War

1880
Elected to US Senate

1886
Loses seat in Senate

1888
Wins presidential election, defeating Cleveland

growing **alliance** between big business and the Republican Party. This alliance is still strong in the United States today.

In office, Benjamin Harrison increased tariffs by signing the *McKinley Tariff Bill*, and he took other pro-business measures. But he also signed the *Sherman Anti-trust Act*, which began to control the vast industrial companies that dominated US industry. Harrison also modernized the navy, reformed the **civil service**, and expanded US naval power in the Pacific Ocean.

NATIVE AMERICANS

⭐ American settlers had fought over land with the Native Americans ever since they first arrived in the country during the 1600s. By the 1880s, the US government had restricted the living areas of Native Americans to a few "Indian reservations."

The final battle between the settlers and the Native Americans took place at Wounded Knee Creek in South Dakota in 1890. Here, 153 members of the Sioux tribe were killed by the US 7th Cavalry. The massacre marked the end of the Native Americans' fight against rule by the US government.

Ceremonial headdress of a Sioux warrior

▲ To celebrate the 400th anniversary of Columbus reaching the Americas, an international exhibition was held in Chicago, with a giant Ferris wheel measuring 250ft (76m) across.

CLEVELAND AGAIN

Harrison tried to get re-elected in 1892, but the country disliked the high tariffs and big business associated with the Republicans. As a result, Grover Cleveland and the **Democratic Party** returned to office. Harrison retired from politics and returned to practice law in Indianapolis, where he died in 1901.

1890
Sioux are defeated at Battle of Wounded Knee

1892
Defeated by Cleveland in presidential election

1901
Dies in Indianapolis, Indiana

1843 Born in Niles, Ohio

1861 Serves in Union army in Civil War

1865 Becomes a lawyer in Ohio

1876 Elected to the House of Representatives

1890 Passes McKinley Tariff Bill through Congress

1890 Loses seat as a result of the McKinley Bill

1891 Elected governor of Ohio

1896 Wins presidential election

1898 US wins war against Spain

In the 1770s, the American colonists fought for their freedom against the British Empire. Just over a century later, their descendants created their own "American Empire." The president who was responsible for this huge growth of power and extension of US lands was William McKinley. Like many presidents, McKinley trained as a lawyer before entering politics as a **Republican** in 1876. He was a friend of the big business executives and in 1890 pushed through **Congress** the *McKinley Tariff Bill*, which raised a range of **taxes** on imported goods. But this success lost him his seat in Congress as anti-**tariff Democrats** swept to power. McKinley returned to his native Ohio, where he served two terms as governor. In 1896 McKinley became his party's presidential candidate.

TERM
1897–1901

PARTY
Republican

VICE-PRESIDENTS
Garret Hobart, Theodore Roosevelt

FIRST LADY
Ida Saxton

STATES IN THE UNION *45*

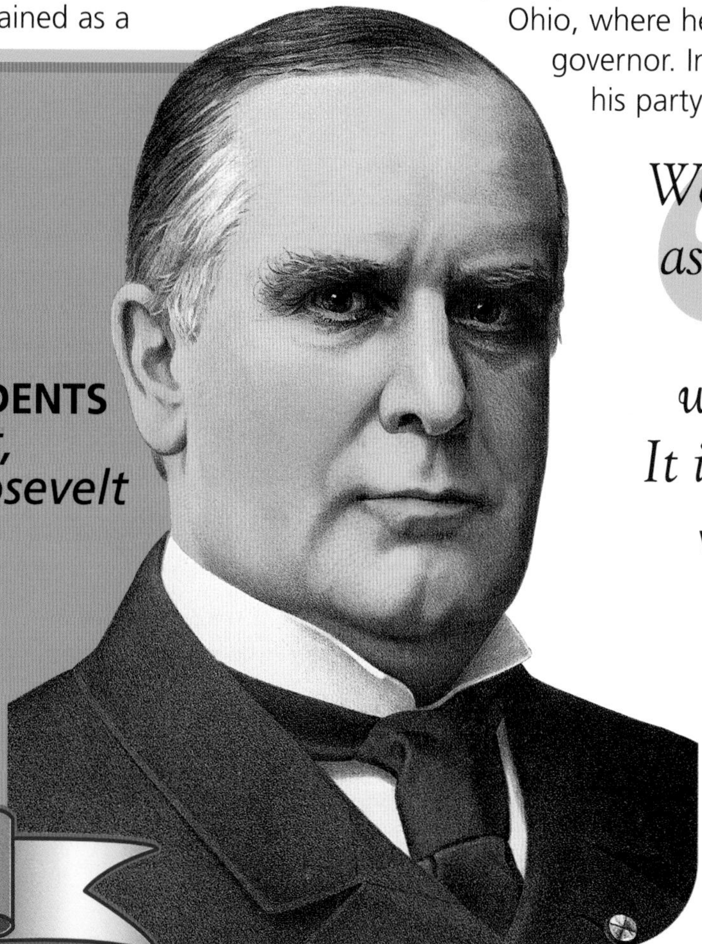

> *We need Hawaii just as much and a good deal more than we did California. It is manifest destiny.*
>
> **WILLIAM MCKINLEY, 1898**

THE WHITE WHITE HOUSE
McKinley disliked the color yellow and banned it from the White House. The walls were painted white or a sober color.

25th president

WILLIAM McKINLEY

▶ Ragtime was the most popular music of the day, and songs like *The Entertainer*, composed by Scott Joplin, sold in their millions.

▶ The assassination of McKinley on September 6, 1901 was reported around the world.

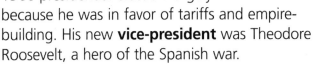

1898
US takes over Hawaii and other Pacific islands

1900
Wins re-election as president

1901
Assassinated at the Pan-American Exposition in Buffalo, New York

▲ The 1898 Spanish-American War ended with victory for the US. Only 298 soldiers died in battle, although another 4,000 died of disease, but the US acquired the vast island of Cuba.

His opponent was the Democrat William Bryan, who wanted lower taxes in order to help the country out of **economic depression**. McKinley campaigned in favor of tariffs and won with ease.

THE SPANISH WAR

During the 1890s, the Spanish Empire in the Caribbean and Pacific Ocean was crumbling. Many people demanded that the US intervene and help Cuba in its revolt against Spanish rule, but McKinley refused. In February 1898, the US battleship *Maine* was blown up in Havana Harbor, Cuba. The US blamed Spain for the explosion and declared war. Within five months, Spain was defeated and its Caribbean and Pacific Empire was taken over by the US. The US also acquired land in Hawaii and Samoa. In addition, US forces were sent to China to crush a rebellion against European and US control. The US was now a major world power. McKinley won the 1900 presidential election largely because he was in favor of tariffs and empire-building. His new **vice-president** was Theodore Roosevelt, a hero of the Spanish war.

A few months after McKinley was re-elected, he began to change his mind on tariffs. He preferred to work out commercial **treaties** between nations in order to lower tariffs and to give the US a market for exports. He took this message to the Pan-American Exposition in New York State in 1901.

At the Exposition, McKinley was shot by a Polish anarchist, Leon Czolgosz, and died a week later. He was the third president to be assassinated in office but, unlike his predecessors, his vice-president was very able to take over his job.

THE AMERICAN EMPIRE

☆ As a result of the five-month war against Spain in 1898 the US acquired Puerto Rico, the Philippines, the island of Guam, and control over Cuba too. Spain's empire in the Americas and the Pacific Ocean came to an end.

☆ In the same year the US took over Hawaii and in 1899 it divided Samoa with Germany. America was now a major economic power in both the Caribbean Sea and the Pacific Ocean.

THEODORE ROOSEVELT

26th president

⭐ **TERM**
1901–1909

⭐ **PARTY**
Republican

⭐ **VICE-PRESIDENT**
Charles Fairbanks

⭐ **FIRST LADY**
Edith Carow

⭐ **STATES IN THE UNION** *46*

> *Speak softly and carry a big stick – you will go far.*

THEODORE ROOSEVELT, 1901

MODERN PRESIDENT
While in office, Roosevelt became the first president to go up in an aeroplane and down in a submarine, the first to visit a foreign country, and the first to ride in a car.

When Theodore Roosevelt became vice-president to William McKinley, one fellow Republican stated: "Don't any of you realize that there's only one life between that madman and the presidency?" A few months later, "that madman" became president. Theodore Roosevelt turned out to be one of the most remarkable presidents that the US has ever known. He left Harvard University in 1880 and within two years was elected as a **Republican** to the New York **state assembly**. There he made a name for himself because

he liked to bring about **reform** and was not afraid to challenge his own party if he thought he was right. In 1889 Roosevelt was called to Washington to join the **Civil Service Commission**. He became New York City police commissioner and was very successful at getting rid of corruption. By 1897 Roosevelt was in the government as the assistant Navy secretary.

THE ACTION MAN
Roosevelt enjoyed the challenge of war and, as soon as fighting broke out with Spain in 1898, he went to Cuba. He returned a hero and went into political office as governor of New York. He continued to encourage changes in his party's ideas.

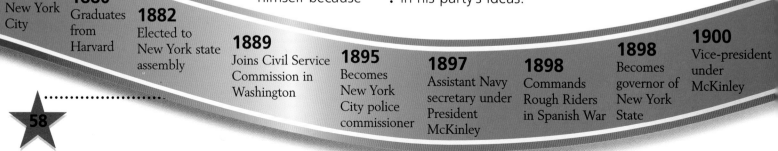

1858
Born in New York City

1880
Graduates from Harvard

1882
Elected to New York state assembly

1889
Joins Civil Service Commission in Washington

1895
Becomes New York City police commissioner

1897
Assistant Navy secretary under President McKinley

1898
Commands Rough Riders in Spanish War

1898
Becomes governor of New York State

1900
Vice-president under McKinley

◀ Roosevelt was fond of hunting wild animals. But his refusal to kill a bear cub started a craze in toy bears named after him, and the first "Teddy" bears were sold.

Roosevelt attacked big business and corruption and tried to help the poor. Many Republicans did not like his policies and arranged for him to become **vice-president** to McKinley in 1900 in order to remove Roosevelt from active politics in New York. After McKinley was assassinated, Roosevelt became president.

ATTACKING BIG BUSINESS

Roosevelt was a powerful and energetic president. He fought big business by regulating its activities, so that business was kept under the control of government. He created the Department of Commerce and Labor to regulate industry and set up laws to control the food and drugs industries and the railroads. He reorganized the Forest Service, and vastly increased the number of national parks and nature reserves. His only failure in the US came when he tried to create a multiracial Republican Party in the southern states. Many members of his own party were against this idea.

In 1903 Colombia rejected the US idea of building a canal across its northern province of Panama in central America. Roosevelt encouraged Panama to fight Colombia and become an independent state, allowing the US to build, and later control, the Panama Canal.

In 1904 war broke out between Russia and Japan. Roosevelt negotiated the peace **treaty** between the two countries in 1905 and gained the **Nobel Peace Prize**. America was now on its way to becoming the richest, most powerful, and important nation on Earth. To show off its strength, Roosevelt sent the US Navy – called the Great White Fleet – on a world cruise in 1907.

In 1909 Roosevelt handed the presidency over to William Taft, the successor that he chose himself. But Taft was not happy being president and, in 1912, Roosevelt challenged him for the Republican presidential nomination. Roosevelt lost, so he stood as an **Independent Progressive candidate**. Some Republican supporters voted for Roosevelt and some for Taft, which split the number of votes for the party. The **Democratic Party** won the election.

Roosevelt was a modern politician, but his own Republican Party did not support his policies. He left an impression on US politics and government that was to last for many years.

THE "ROUGH RIDER"

☆ Roosevelt gained his reputation as an action man during the Spanish War when he commanded his own cavalry regiment, the Rough Riders. They distinguished themselves in the Battle of San Juan Heights, a strategic hill overlooking the Cuban port of Santiago.

San Juan Heights, Cuba

1901
Becomes president when McKinley is assassinated

1904
Wins re-election as president

1905
Wins Nobel Peace Prize

1909
Steps down as president

1912
Fights for the presidency as an Independent

1919
Dies in Oyster Bay, New York

◀ In December 1903, the Wright Brothers became the first people to fly an aeroplane. They flew over Kitty Hawk, North Carolina.

William Taft didn't really want to be president at all and hated politics. His first and last love was law. After Taft graduated from Yale University, he gained a law degree from school in his home town, Cincinnati. A series of law jobs in the Ohio state government gained him a good reputation both as a lawyer and as an administrator.

In 1890 he became US **solicitor general** in the government of President Benjamin Harrison and then a circuit judge. In 1898 the US conquered the Philippines. Taft was appointed civil governor of the colony in 1900 and brought it peace.

The people of the Philippines wanted independence, but Taft worked hard to convince them that being part of the US was a good thing. He built schools, roads, and irrigation projects and sold land cheaply to poor farmers to help them become richer.

On his return to Washington in 1904, he became secretary of war and, in 1908, Roosevelt chose him as the Republican presidential candidate.

AN UNHAPPY PRESIDENT

Taft won the 1908 general election by a **landslide**. He carried on Roosevelt's work against the powerful industrial companies and supported the workers and the poor. During his presidency, two changes were made to the **Constitution**. One of these set a **federal** income **tax**. The other allowed for **senators** to be elected by the people for the first time.

But Taft did not enjoy politics – he described the White House as "the lonesomest place in the world" and stated that politics made him sick. Roosevelt turned against Taft and fought him for the Republican presidential nomination in 1912.

> *I would rather be chief justice of the United States, and enjoy a quieter life than that which comes with the White House.*
>
> **WILLIAM TAFT, 1910**

☆ **TERM**
1909–1913

☆ **PARTY**
Republican

☆ **VICE-PRESIDENT**
James Sherman

☆ **FIRST LADY**
Helen Herron

☆ **STATES IN THE UNION** *48*

27th president

WILLIAM TAFT

1857
Born in Cincinnati, Ohio

1878
Graduates from Yale University

1880
Gains law degree

STARS AND STRIPES NAILED TO THE "NORTH POLE."

DR. FREDERICK A. COOK
APRIL 21 1908.

COMMANDER ROBERT E. PEARY.
APRIL 6. 1909.

TWO DAUNTLESS AMERICANS WHO REACHED THE GOAL OF A THOUSAND YEARS AND PLANTED THE STARS AND STRIPES UPON THE AXIS OF THE WORLD.

◀ On April 6, 1909, the US explorer Robert Peary and his African-American companion, Matthew Henson, claimed to be the first people to reach the North Pole. Frederick Cook made the same claim a year earlier, on April 21, 1908.

When Roosevelt lost the party nomination, he decided to run for president as an **Independent**, gaining 88 **Electoral College** votes to Taft's miserable eight. The winner of that election, Woodrow Wilson, gained a total of 435 votes.

BACK TO THE LAW

At this point, Taft retired to teach law at Yale University. In 1921 his dream came true when the Republican president Warren Harding appointed him chief justice. He held the job until his death nine years later. During his time as chief justice, Taft proved that he was a cautious but capable judge. He is the only man to have held both the top political and the top legal job in the United States of America, that of president and chief justice of the US **Supreme Court**.

THE BIG PRESIDENT

☆ William Taft weighed 332lbs (150kg) and was the largest US president in history. But he did not "throw his weight around" while he was president. In fact, he liked to make jokes about his size and was a good-natured man with an "infectious chuckle."

▶ On the night of April 14, 1912, the luxury liner *Titanic* was half-way across the North Atlantic Ocean on its maiden voyage between England and New York. The ship struck an iceberg and sank beneath the waves, killing 1,517 people.

1890
Becomes US solicitor general

1892
Appointed US judge

1900
Governor of the Philippines

1904
US secretary of state for war

1908
Elected president

1912
Defeated by Wilson

1921
Chief justice of US Supreme Court

1930
Dies in Washington, D.C.

◀ Jack Johnson was the first Black American heavyweight champion of the world. He held the title during 1908–15.

WOODROW WILSON

⭐ **TERM**
1913–1921

⭐ **PARTY**
Democrat

⭐ **VICE-PRESIDENT**
Thomas Marshall

⭐ **FIRST LADIES**
Ellen Axson,
Edith Galt

⭐ **STATES IN**
THE UNION *48*

The world must be made safe for democracy.

WOODROW WILSON, 1917

LAWN GRAZING
During World War I, Wilson kept a flock of sheep at the White House to keep the lawns under control. He liked to wander outside and pat their heads.

President Woodrow Wilson had two successful careers. The first, and the longest, was as an academic and writer of books about politics and government. The second career was as president of a country at war, and this job brought him international fame.

Wilson was a slow learner to begin with and did not make sense of the alphabet until he was nine. He made up for lost time by studying at Princeton University and taking a law degree at the University of Virginia. After a year as a lawyer

in Atlanta, Georgia, he returned to academic life, first at Johns Hopkins University and then at Princeton. He became president of Princeton, where he changed and modernized the way it taught its students. Wilson's work in Princeton influenced university education across America. But he made enemies and, in 1910, he was forced to resign.

INTO POLITICS
Wilson then changed career. He ran as the **Democratic** candidate for governor of New Jersey and won the election. As governor, he introduced many **reforms**. These made him famous and, in 1912, he was his party's candidate for president. Although he had more experience at academic debate, Wilson was a good **campaigner**.

1856
Born in Staunton, Virginia

1879
Graduates from Princeton University

1882
Qualifies as a lawyer at the University of Virginia

1883
Studies for a PhD from Johns Hopkins University

1890
Professor of law and politics at Princeton University

1910
Elected governor of New Jersey

1912
Elected president

1914
World War I breaks out in Europe

WORLD WAR I

⭐ War broke out in Europe in 1914, after the assassination of the heir to the Austrian throne. Britain, France, and Russia were on one side, Germany, Austro-Hungary, and Ottoman Turkey were on the other. In 1917 Germany began to attack US shipping to prevent it from supplying Britain with food and other materials. The US declared war on Germany and sent troops to fight in Europe. The arrival of the US troops helped Britain and her Allies win the War in 1918.

US troops in Europe in 1918

He promised a "**New Freedom**" in the US, which would improve welfare for poor people and conditions for working people. Theodore Roosevelt promised a "**New Nationalism**" and President Taft's **Republican** policies offered no change. Wilson won the election with ease.

Wilson lowered **tariffs** to encourage trade and set the first **federal** income **tax** to raise money for the government. He supported the trade unions and made strikes legal. He also approved the *Adamson Act*, which meant that

railroad workers could not be forced to work more than eight hours a day. Other workers then gained the same privilege. Wilson also restricted the use of children as workers in factories and mines.

THE PEACEMAKER

As president, Wilson was a campaigner for peace. He tried to keep the USA out of overseas battles, and avoided war with Mexico, which was in the middle of a violent revolution. When Germany sank the ocean liner *Lusitania* in 1915, killing more than 100 US citizens, Wilson refused to go to war. In 1916 he was re-elected and in 1917 he was forced to join World War I when Germany attacked US ships in the Atlantic Ocean.

After the war with Germany, Wilson worked hard to create a lasting peace. In 1918 he proposed a world peace **treaty**, called the Fourteen Points, and suggested that an international organization be formed to help settle arguments between countries. It was called the **League of Nations**. In 1920 Wilson was awarded the **Nobel Peace Prize** for his peacekeeping efforts. But, in the same year, the US **Senate** refused to agree to the treaty or to allow the US to join the League of Nations. This was a serious defeat for Wilson, and he retired from the presidency a broken man.

▶ The world's first jazz record was made in 1917. Soon, jazz music was very popular in the US. Most jazz bands originated in New Orleans.

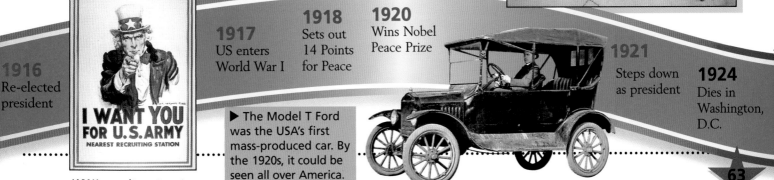

1916 Re-elected president

1917 US enters World War I

1918 Sets out 14 Points for Peace

1920 Wins Nobel Peace Prize

1921 Steps down as president

1924 Dies in Washington, D.C.

I WANT YOU FOR U.S. ARMY
NEAREST RECRUITING STATION

WW1 recruitment poster

▶ The Model T Ford was the USA's first mass-produced car. By the 1920s, it could be seen all over America.

63

Warren Harding is said to be at the top of everyone's list of the worst US presidents. He became president almost by accident, and as president, he was surrounded by scandal. Few people mourned his early death.

LUCKY BREAK

Harding was born in Ohio and, after attending the local college, had a number of different jobs. During this time he failed to become a lawyer, sold insurance too cheaply and was fired, taught in school and hated it, sold hardware, played the cornet in a band, and ended up as a journalist.

His wife, Florence, was very ambitious, and she encouraged him to follow a political career. He was elected as a **Republican** to the Ohio **state assembly** and, in 1914, got to the US **Senate**, where he did not achieve very much. Warren Harding's "big break" came during World War I. He proposed a congressional **bill** that would have allowed Theodore Roosevelt, the former president, to raise a volunteer army. The bill did not become law, but Roosevelt appreciated Harding's support and asked Harding to be his **running mate** in the next presidential election. When Roosevelt died suddenly, Harding won the presidential nomination himself and was elected president in 1920.

THE GAMBLER
Harding played poker in the White House and gambled away some of its china. He also drank bootleg liquor, even though it was banned.

THE SCANDALOUS YEARS

After the war years, Americans wanted a return to normality, or "normalcy" as Harding called it. Harding took advantage of this wish, stating that he and Florence were "just plain folks." He won the election by a **landslide**. But once Harding became president, his lack

> *We must stabilize and strive for normalcy.*
>
> **WARREN HARDING, 1920**

☆ **TERM**
1921–1923

☆ **PARTY**
Republican

☆ **VICE-PRESIDENT**
Calvin Coolidge

☆ **FIRST LADY**
Florence de Wolfe

☆ **STATES IN THE UNION** *48*

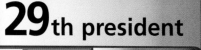

29th president

WARREN HARDING

1865 Born in Corsica, Ohio

1879 Studies at Ohio Central College

1884 Becomes partner in the Marion Daily Star newspape

The scandal over the Teapot Dome oilfield in Wyoming revealed a high level of corruption in the Harding government. After a Senate investigation into the event, many politicians were forced to resign.

PROHIBITION

On January 16, 1920, the manufacture, sale, import, and export of alcohol was banned in America. This was known as "Prohibition," because any contact with alcoholic drink was prohibited and gallons of alcohol were poured away. These laws were established by the 18th Amendment to the Constitution, which introduced Prohibition and stayed in place until 1933. Many people ignored Prohibition and openly disobeyed the law. People drank alcohol in illegal bars called "speakeasies." Gangsters got rich by importing illegal alcohol, known as bootleg liquor. In the end, Prohibition failed, because instead of decreasing the drinking of alcohol, it increased crime.

Bootleg liquor is emptied into the gutter

of ability was discovered. "I know how far removed from greatness I am," he stated. He proved that this statement was true, as he did little good as president. He did not like to get involved in problems unless it was absolutely necessary. His policies supported big business and high **tariffs**. This was a complete change from the **interventionist** approach of both Theodore Roosevelt and Woodrow Wilson. Harding was not a good manager, and he appointed some corrupt people to his government.

This move proved to be fatal for those involved. In 1923 two of his colleagues killed themselves when rumors about their behavior spread. As Harding went on a tour of the US, a huge scandal broke out. Some of his **Cabinet** members had taken money from oil companies in exchange for allowing the companies to exploit the Teapot Dome oilfield. As a result of the scandal, Harding collapsed and soon died, leaving other people to fix these problems.

1891
Marries Florence de Wolfe

1899
Elected to Ohio state assembly

1904
Lieutenant governor of Ohio

1910
Fails to be elected governor

1914
Elected to US Senate

1920
Elected president

1923
Dies in San Francisco, California

This is the great picture upon which the famous comedian has worked a whole year.
6 reels of Joy.

Charles Chaplin in "THE KID"

The 1920s was the age of the silent picture. Millions of people went "to the movies" to see stars such as Charlie Chaplin.

Although he was a man of few words, Calvin Coolidge became famous when he made a statement as governor of Massachusetts in 1919. When the Boston police force went on strike Coolidge sent in the state **militia** to crush the strike. "There is no right to strike against the public safety by anybody, anywhere, any time," he said. His words were heard and appreciated across the nation, and his **Republican Party** chose him as **vice-presidential** candidate to Warren Harding. When President Harding died unexpectedly in 1923, Calvin Coolidge was sworn in as the new president.

IN HIS OWN LIGHT

Like many other presidents, Coolidge trained as a lawyer and worked in city and state politics first, ending up as state governor. He was given the presidential **oath of office** by lantern light at his father's home in Vermont. He arrived in Washington determined to end the corruption of Harding's **Cabinet** and to win his own re-election.

☆ **TERM**
1923–1929

☆ **PARTY**
Republican

☆ **VICE-PRESIDENT**
Charles Dawes

☆ **FIRST LADY**
Grace Goodhue

☆ **STATES IN THE UNION** *48*

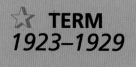

30th president

> *The chief business of the American people is business.*
>
> **CALVIN COOLIDGE, 1925**

A DARK HORSE
Calvin Coolidge was not as quiet as he seemed. He kept a pet racoon and rode an electrical rocking horse most days, whooping like a cowboy.

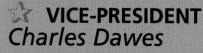

CALVIN COOLIDGE

1920
Elected
vice-president to
Warren Harding

1923
Becomes president on
death of Harding

1924
Wins re-election
as president

▶ In 1929 the first Academy Award
was given by the Academy of
Motion Picture Arts and Sciences.

1929
Steps down from
the White House

1933
Dies in
Northampton,
Massachusetts

◀ In 1927, Charles Lindbergh was the first person to fly single-handedly across the Atlantic Ocean. His flight from New York City to Paris, France, took 33 hours, 29 minutes.

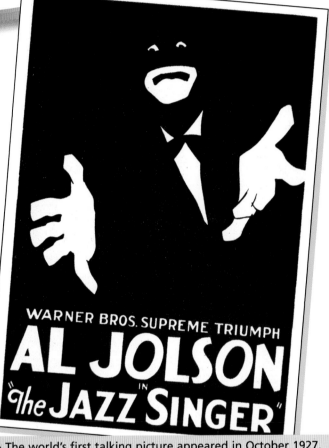

▲ The world's first talking picture appeared in October 1927. *The Jazz Singer* starred Al Jolson and included spoken words for the first time. Until then, movie-goers could hear only sound effects and background music.

A LIGHT TOUCH

Coolidge was a typical conservative Republican. This meant that he believed in letting business get on with the business of making money, and he was opposed to the state getting involved in helping poor farmers, or helping anyone else. He preached that the less the government got involved, the better for everyone. The country was getting very rich after the war, and Coolidge just allowed it to get richer, keeping quietly out of the way.

He reduced **taxes** and the **national debt**, encouraged people to invest in the stock exchange, and worked hard for peace abroad. But in the next decade, it turned out that some of these decisions were the wrong ones for the US.

At the time, however, President Coolidge easily won the presidential election of 1924 and could have won again in 1928 if he had wanted to carry on as president. Instead, he announced his retirement from politics, and settled down to write a book about his life. He died peacefully in his beloved town of Northampton, Massachusetts.

THE SILENT ONE

☆ Coolidge hardly spoke, and when he did, he said only a few words. He was nicknamed "Silent Cal" and when he died, the American writer, Dorothy Parker, remarked: "How do they know?" A number of other people are said to have made the same comment.

HERBERT HOOVER

⭐ **TERM**
1929–1933

⭐ **PARTY**
Republican

⭐ **VICE-PRESIDENT**
Charles Curtis

⭐ **FIRST LADY**
Lou Henry

⭐ **STATES IN
THE UNION** *48*

> *...a chicken in every pot, a car in every garage.*

HERBERT HOOVER, 1928

THE WESTERNER
Herbert Hoover was the first president to be born west of the Mississippi River. He was also the first Quaker to be president.

Herbert Clark Hoover **was one of the most qualified men to become president. He had worked hard and become a millionaire, and he** was very good at administration. He also had been successful in government. Unfortunately, his period in office coincided with the greatest **economic depression** in American history and Hoover did not manage this crisis well.

Hoover began with nothing in life. His parents died before he was nine, and he was brought up by his uncle – a Quaker doctor – and his aunt in Oregon. He left high school at 14 to work as an office boy. He later became interested in engineering and graduated from Stanford University with a degree in mining engineering. In 1908 he set up his own mining consultancy company, which made him very rich.

Hoover was in London, England, when war broke out in Europe in 1914. He chaired the American Relief Commission, which helped the 150,000 Americans caught up in World War I to get back home safely. When the US entered the war in 1917, Hoover ran a number of American organizations that helped victims of war and sent food to the millions of people in Russia who did not have enough to eat.

1874
Born in West Branch, Iowa

1895
Graduates from Stanford University

1914
Becomes chair of American Relief Committee in Europe

1917
Becomes US food administrator

1921
Secretary of commerce under Harding, then Coolidge

1928
Elected president

1929
Great Depression begins

▲ The New York Stock Exchange on Wall Street was the busiest stock exchange in the world. Here investors bought and sold stocks and shares in US companies and received a dividend, or share of the profits, when the company did well.

INTO GOVERNMENT

Hoover's work during the war brought him to the attention of President Harding, who made him **secretary of commerce**. He continued to hold this post under President Coolidge. In this job, Hoover worked with companies to set safety standards for workers, and safety rules for automobiles and railroads. He also helped the new airlines to get started. President Hoover began a series of building projects, including the Boulder Dam, which was later re-named the Hoover Dam in his honor.

Hoover was the natural choice to succeed Calvin Coolidge as president. He promised prosperity for all and believed that the rich period of the 1920s would continue forever. The Wall Street Crash ended such dreams.

Hoover did not like the government to take too much control. He took little action to solve the problem other than to cut taxes and encourage business in the hope that the **Great Depression** would solve itself. It did not. Many people blamed Hoover because they were unemployed and poor. As a result, he became extremely unpopular.

A NEW CAREER

Hoover eventually realized that something had to be done to stop the Depression, so he set up an organization to help industry. But this turned out to be too little, too late. Hoover was beaten in the presidential election by Franklin Roosevelt.

Hoover retired from public life. Then, in 1946, he once again organized food supplies to war victims in Europe. In 1947 and again in 1953, he headed the **Federal** Hoover Commissions. These groups helped the government to manage the new US, which was rich and powerful after World War I.

THE GREAT DEPRESSION

☆ During the 1920s, the value of company shares rose steadily on the New York Stock Exchange and American people became wealthy. On October 29, 1929, the stock market crashed. Share prices, and therefore the value of US companies and goods, fell heavily. As a result, the US economy collapsed and, by 1933, America was producing half what it did in 1929. By 1933, during the Great Depression, about 13 million people were unemployed (one in four of the working population). Farmers lost their land, people lost their savings, and the nation was in ruins.

Unemployed people line up for free food

1932
Loses presidential election to Roosevelt

1947, 1953
Heads Hoover commissions into government reform

1964
Dies in New York City

◄ The Empire State Building, the world's tallest skyscraper at that time, opened in New York City in May 1931. It is 1,245ft (380m) tall and has 86 floors.

1882
Born in Hyde Park, New York

1904
Graduates from Harvard and becomes a lawyer

1910
Elected to the New York Senate

1913
Assistant secretary of the Navy under President Wilson

1920
Runs as vice-presidential candidate but loses election

1921
Struck down with polio

1928
Elected governor of New York

◀ In the 1930s farms in the Midwest were lost under dust blown by strong winds. The area was known as the Dust Bowl.

STUCK IN
To relax from the pressures of work, Roosevelt liked to organize his collection of 25,000 postage stamps, which he had collected into 40 albums.

In a time of great need, as millions of Americans lost their jobs and homes, the country elected an outstanding president.

Franklin Delano Roosevelt served for longer than any other US president, including his distant relative, Theodore Roosevelt. He brought hope to millions of people and helped the nation through the **Great Depression** and World War II.

Roosevelt practiced as a lawyer, but he realized that he was more interested in politics. He became active in the **Democratic Party** and was elected to the New York **State Senate** in 1910. President Wilson made him assistant secretary of the Navy in 1913, a position that he held throughout the war. In 1920 he was the **vice-presidential** candidate with James Cox, but lost to the **Republicans** Warren Harding and Calvin Coolidge. Despite this defeat, Roosevelt's future looked promising. But, in 1921, he became disabled by polio and was confined to a wheelchair.

☆ **TERM**
1933–1945

☆ **PARTY**
Democrat

☆ **VICE-PRESIDENTS**
*John Garner,
Henry Wallace,
Harry Truman*

☆ **FIRST LADY**
Eleanor Roosevelt

☆ **STATES IN THE UNION** *48*

32nd president

The only thing we have to fear is fear itself.

INAUGURAL ADDRESS, 1933

FRANKLIN ROOSEVELT

▶ US and Allied troops land on the French coast on D-Day, June 6, 1944.

1932
Elected president

1936 & 1940
Re-elected president

1941
USA enters World War II

1944
Re-elected president

1945
Dies in Warm Springs, Georgia

FEISTY FIRST LADY

Eleanor Roosevelt, the niece of President Theodore Roosevelt, was also famous. She was concerned with helping poor people and those who were badly treated, and helped to write the Universal Declaration of Human Rights in 1948.

Many people thought his public life would be over, but Roosevelt disagreed. He fought back and won election as governor of New York in 1928. He was a good administrator and introduced many popular **reforms** in the state. In 1932 he ran for president. As the Great Depression got worse, Roosevelt promised to make the people of America rich once again. He called this "the new deal for the American people." This promise helped him to defeat President Hoover in the presidential election by a **landslide** victory.

THE NEW DEAL

At his **inauguration** in 1933, Roosevelt stated that the only thing the country had to fear was "fear itself." He was very active and made changes straight away. Within 99 days of becoming president, he had made major reforms in US government. These changes, known as the **New Deal**, set the US on the road to recovery. The financial and economic systems were transformed. The poor were given assistance, the elderly received pensions for the first time, and programs were provided to help the unemployed find work. Not all Roosevelt's measures worked, but they gave the American people new hope for the future.

WORLD LEADER

Throughout his presidency, Roosevelt spoke to his nation on the radio in regular "fireside chats." These talks reassured people and made Roosevelt very popular. As a result of this popularity, Roosevelt was re-elected as president a total of three times.

During the war, Roosevelt played a major role in supporting the army and reassuring the American people. Along with Winston Churchill of Britain and Josef Stalin of Russia, Roosevelt planned for the future of the world after the war had ended. But because Roosevelt got so heavily involved in world events, his hard work started to harm his health. In April 1945, Roosevelt died suddenly, very close to the end of the war. On his death, Americans knew that they had seen a time when one of the most remarkable men who ever lived had been their president.

WORLD WAR II

In 1939 Nazi Germany invaded Poland, so Britain and France declared war on Germany. World War II broke out in Europe. At first, the US did not take sides in the war, although it agreed to lend ships and other military equipment to Britain. In return, Britain let the US use some of its military bases. On December 7, 1941, Japanese airplanes bombed the US naval base, Pearl Harbor, in Hawaii. This forced the US to declare war on Japan and Germany. Millions of Americans fought in the war with Britons and Russians, until Germany and Japan were defeated in 1945.

Japan attacks Pearl Harbor

1884
Born in Lamar, Missouri

1906
Takes over family farm

1917
Fights in France during World War I

1934
Elected to Senate

1944
Chosen as vice-president by Roosevelt

1945
Becomes president on Roosevelt's death

1945
US drops two atomic bombs on Japan to end war

▶ The world's first atomic bomb was dropped on the Japanese city of Hiroshima on August 6, 1945.

To most people, Harry Truman did not seem like a potential president. But when Truman took over from Roosevelt in 1945, he surprised the world with his ability and skill as leader of the country.

Harry Truman was born on a farm in Missouri. He did not go to college, but he held a number of jobs before he took over the farm's management. During World War I, he enlisted in the army and fought in France.

On his return from France, he married Bess Wallace and opened a men's clothing store. The store failed, so in 1922 he became a **Democratic** politician in Missouri. He was an honest and hard-working politician and, in 1934, Truman was elected to the US **Senate**.

Truman was a good **senator**. In 1941 he was appointed chair of a committee that reviewed America's national defense. The committee's suggestions saved huge sums of money and improved the production of war materials. It was a great success and became known as the Truman Committee.

☆ **TERM**
1945–1953

☆ **PARTY**
Democrat

☆ **VICE-PRESIDENT**
Alben Barkley

☆ **FIRST LADY**
Bess Wallace

☆ **STATES IN THE UNION** *48*

33rd president

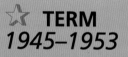

The buck stops here.

MOTTO ON TRUMAN'S DESK

THE SILENT "S"
Harry Truman's middle initial was "S". The letter did not stand for any name, but both his grandfathers thought he was named after them!

HARRY TRUMAN

1948
Wins second term as president

1950
Sends US troops to fight in Korea

1953
Steps down as president

1972
Dies in Kansas City, Missouri

NOT A GOOD START

☆ Truman was clever enough to go to college, but did not because his father, a farmer, had no money. Truman's poor eyesight meant that he could not go to military academy either. He spent his childhood playing the piano and wanted to be a concert pianist, but his parents could not afford to pay for lessons. As president, he had three pianos in the White House.

▲ Almost every American expected Harry Truman to lose the 1948 presidential election, and one newspaper – the *Chicago Daily Tribune* – even put a headline on the front page saying he was defeated. In fact, Truman won the election with ease!

Truman was chosen by Roosevelt as his **vice-presidential running mate** in 1944. Truman did not get on well with Roosevelt, but nonetheless, they won the election. Then, after only 83 days, Roosevelt died, so Truman took over the top job.

SURPRISE PRESIDENT

At the time, World War II was still being fought. The war with Germany was almost over, but the war with Japan continued. One of Truman's first jobs as president was to decide whether to drop two atomic bombs on the Japanese cities of Hiroshima and Nagasaki. He chose to use the bombs and brought the war to an end in 1945.

Truman dealt quickly with the problems of the post-war world. He promised US aid to war-torn Europe and countries fighting **Communism**.

Truman passed laws to stop **discrimination** against African-Americans. The US was now in a period of expansion, full employment, and growing prosperity. In 1948 Truman decided to seek re-election as president. He was opposed by two candidates from his own party. These were the pro-discrimination South Carolina governor, Strom Thurmond, and Roosevelt's former vice-president, Henry Wallace. The **Republicans** were expected to win. But, to everyone's surprise, Truman was returned for a second term.

A NEW VIEW

The US and the USSR had been on the same side in World War II, but were rivals by the end of the 1940s. The two never had any physical battles, but fought a **Cold War** in Europe, Asia, and later, Africa. In 1949 Truman took the US into the **North Atlantic Treaty Organization (NATO)**, which tied the USA and Western Europe together for security against the Russian-dominated Eastern Europe. In 1950 he sent US troops to fight in the war that broke out when Communist North Korea invaded US-backed South Korea.

By the time Truman left office in 1953, most people had changed their view of the president. He had been dismissed as "a little man," but many now realized that he was tougher and far cleverer than they had thought. In getting the US through all the difficulties that it met after 1945, Truman proved himself to be just as capable and far-sighted as his much-admired predecessor, Roosevelt.

DWIGHT EISENHOWER

★ **TERM**
1953–1961

★ **PARTY**
Republican

★ **VICE-PRESIDENT**
Richard Nixon

★ **FIRST LADY**
Mamie Doud

★ **STATES IN THE UNION** *50*

> *...people want peace so much that one of these days governments had better get out of the way and let them have it.*

DWIGHT EISENHOWER, 1959

CAMP DAVID

Dwight Eisenhower was devoted to his grandson, David. Eisenhower renamed Shangri-la, the presidential retreat in Maryland, Camp David, in his honor.

Like many presidents before him, Dwight David Eisenhower was a wartime hero who became president. And like them, he was first and foremost a soldier. His politics were conservative and cautious and he could have fitted into either political party. He appeared casual, but his appearance hid a strong ambition.

Dwight Eisenhower was born in Texas but, at the age of two, his family moved to Kansas. He went to the West Point Military Academy, where he played football until an injury stopped him. He stayed in the US during World War I, training tank battalions. His career really took off when he graduated first out of a class of 275 from the Command and General School at Fort Leavenworth, Kansas. From then on his progress was rapid. By June 1942, six months after the US had entered World War II, Eisenhower beat 366 senior army officers to become commander-general of the US forces in Europe. In that job, he organized Operation Overlord – the campaign to free Europe from Nazi Germany. In June 1944, he commanded the largest-ever seaborne invasion in history, the **D-Day Landings** on the Normandy beaches in France.

1890
Born in Denison, Texas

1915
Graduates from West Point Military Academy

1933
Becomes aide to General Douglas MacArthur, US Army chief of staff

1941
Promoted to brigadier-general

1942
Commander, US forces in Europe

1944
Leads D-Day invasion

1945
Becomes chief of staff, US Army

POST-WAR SERVICE

By now Ike, as he was commonly known, was famous. He was not a daring leader, but he attracted loyalty from his troops and was good at keeping the US, French, and British generals who reported to him under control.

When the war ended in 1945, Eisenhower wanted to retire, but instead he was made chief of staff of the US Army. Eisenhower oversaw the task of reorganizing the vast army for peace. In 1948 he left the army to become president of Columbia University in New York. But, in 1949, Ike was back in the army, as head of the new **North Atlantic Treaty Organization (NATO)**.

WAR AND PEACE

At this point, Eisenhower considered a career in politics. Both political parties approached him to be their candidate for the election. In 1952 he ran for the **Republican Party**'s nomination. He won on the first **ballot** and, in November 1952, was elected president.

EASY-GOING IKE

☆ The Eisenhowers moved house 35 times in the first 35 years of their marriage, but Mamie Eisenhower never complained. "I have only one career, and his name is Ike," she said.

☆ Ike took up oil painting as a good way to relax and be alone. He also played golf, so much so that the US Golf Association built a course for him near the White House.

General "Ike" Eisenhower

Eisenhower promised to go to Korea to break the deadlock in the war, and a **truce** was signed in July 1953.

There were growing racial problems in the US at this time. African-Americans were demanding their civil rights. Eisenhower ended **segregation** in education, but did little else to support **civil rights**.

The rivalry between the USSR and the USA continued. Eisenhower increased the number of nuclear weapons in the US and ensured that his country kept a stronger army and more weapons than the Russians. The launch by the USSR of the world's first satellite in space in 1957 was a severe blow to the US, which wanted to be the first country to do this.

America struggled to deal with the age of nuclear weapons and the power of Russia. But Eisenhower's firm yet friendly leadership and his relaxed style reassured the American people that all was well in the world, and that the US was still strong.

THE SPACE RACE

☆ In 1957, the USSR sent the world's first-ever artificial satellite into space. It was called *Sputnik I*. In 1961, the Russians sent the first astronaut into space. The first person to walk on the Moon was the American, Neil Armstrong, in 1969.

Yuri Gagarin, the first man in space

1949
Appointed supreme commander of NATO

1953
Elected president

1957
Re-elected president

1959
Alaska and Hawaii join the Union

1961
Steps down from the White House

1969
Dies in Washington, D.C.

▲ Senator Joseph McCarthy, who led the attack on suspected American Communists in the 1950s.

▲ Rock and roll music made its debut in the 1950s when Elvis Presley had his first No. 1 record.

John Fitzgerald Kennedy was a hugely popular leader, even though he was president for less than three years. He was the first US president to be born in the 20th century and one of the youngest ever elected. He was also handsome, with a glamorous wife and young family. As the years have gone by since his death, his reputation has declined. But in the early 1960s, John F. Kennedy was the hope of the world.

Kennedy was born into a large Catholic family. His father, Joseph Kennedy, was once **ambassador** to Britain and was determined that one of his children would become president. John went to Harvard University and then joined the US Navy. As captain of a torpedo boat, he saved his crew when it was sunk by the Japanese in 1943. He was honored for his bravery.

After the war, he entered politics as a **Democrat**. By 1956 he was well-known enough to try to become his party's **vice-presidential** candidate. Four years later he won his party's nomination for president. He beat the **Republican**, Richard Nixon, and became the 35th president of the USA.

A TIME OF CONFLICT

As president, Kennedy governed a nation torn apart over **civil rights**. He set out a program that he called the New Frontier, which would tackle poverty and inequality. He made laws to protect people's civil rights, set up medical care for the aged, and spent money on education. He also promised to get an American on the Moon by the

> *...ask not what your country can do for you – ask what you can do for your country.*

JOHN KENNEDY, 1961

CAMELOT
Kennedy surrounded himself with so many glamorous people that the White House was sometimes compared to Camelot, the court of the mythical English King, Arthur, and his knights of the Round Table.

☆ **TERM**
1961–1963

☆ **PARTY**
Democrat

☆ **VICE-PRESIDENT**
Lyndon Johnson

☆ **FIRST LADY**
Jacqueline Bouvier

☆ **STATES IN THE UNION** *50*

35th president

JOHN KENNEDY

1917
Born in Brookline, Massachusetts

1940
Graduates from Harvard University

◀ Jacqueline Bouvier married John Kennedy in 1953, and often attracted as much attention as he did!

end of the decade. Many of these **reforms** were blocked by **Congress**, but Kennedy gained huge support for his work from African-Americans and the poor. In 1962 Russia placed nuclear missiles on the Caribbean island of Cuba, only a few miles off the US coast. Kennedy ordered the Russians to remove them. For over a week, neither country would back down. Then the Russians gave in. The world had come very close to nuclear war.

In 1963 Kennedy signed a **treaty** with the Russians which banned the testing of nuclear weapons in the atmosphere. Tension between the two countries continued, however, as Kennedy sent support to South Vietnam to stop the country from being invaded by **Communist** North Vietnam.

WHAT IF?

At the end of 1963, Kennedy was one of the most popular presidents in history. His assassination in Dallas was such a shock that the world took many years to discover the truth about Kennedy's presidency. In the years since his death, Kennedy's role in starting the war in Vietnam,

▼The US and the USSR came close to nuclear war in 1962. Here, Kennedy inspects some US weaponry.

CIVIL RIGHTS

☆ John F. Kennedy gave his support to civil rights in the US. Although the Constitution stated that African-Americans had the same rights as white Americans, many still suffered discrimination. From the mid-1950s, African-Americans demonstrated for their civil rights. They held meetings, marched in the streets, and took their case to the courts. The leader of the Civil Rights Movement was a Baptist minister, called Reverend Martin Luther King, Jr. His non-violent campaigns made him a popular figure throughout the world.

his many affairs, and his links with gangsters have tarnished his image. Yet two of his brothers tried for the White House, and the love affair between America and the Kennedy family seems to continue.

THE ASSASSINATION

☆ On November 22, 1963, John F. Kennedy visited Dallas with his wife. Traveling in an open-top car, he was shot dead. Lee Harvey Oswald, a former marine, was arrested for the crime, but two days later he was shot in jail by Jack Ruby, a local nightclub owner. The new president, Lyndon Johnson set up the Warren Commission to find out if Oswald had acted alone or if there had been a conspiracy to kill President Kennedy. The Commission stated that Oswald alone had killed the president, but there are still many theories about who actually killed JFK.

News that shocked the world

CHICAGO DAILY NEWS FINAL MARKETS **RED STREAK**

PRESIDENT IS KILLED
Texas Sniper Escapes; Johnson Sworn In

1941
Joins US Navy

1947
Elected to House of Representatives

1952
Elected to Senate

1956
Fails to become Democratic vice-presidential candidate

1960
Elected president

1962
Confronts Russia over missiles in Cuba

1963
Assassinated in Dallas, Texas

77

LYNDON JOHNSON

36th president

★ **TERM**
1963–1969

★ **PARTY**
Democrat

★ **VICE-PRESIDENT**
Hubert Humphrey

★ **FIRST LADY**
Claudia "Lady Bird" Alta Taylor

★ **STATES IN THE UNION** *50*

> *This administration, today, here and now, declares unconditional war on poverty.*
>
> **LYNDON JOHNSON, 1964**

LBJ x 5
Every member of Lyndon Baines Johnson's family shared his initials: his wife Lady Bird, his daughters, Lynda Bird and Luci Baines, and even his first dog, Little Beagle.

Lyndon B. Johnson's presidency is one of the great tragedies of US history. Johnson had not expected to become president. He made many important changes to the way the country was run and he supported the poor and disadvantaged. But a war divided his country and lost him his job.

Lyndon Johnson was a Texan who trained as a teacher and taught for two years before working for a Texan congressman. In 1935 President Roosevelt made Johnson head of the **New Deal** National Youth Administration in Texas. By 1937 Johnson was in the **House of Representatives**. Eleven years later, he was in the **Senate**.

Johnson was committed to the ideals of Roosevelt's New Deal and pushed through many new laws. He led the fight for the 1957 and 1960 *Civil Rights Acts* and supported social **welfare** and other programs that helped the less fortunate in society. Johnson was also good at fixing political and social problems. As a result, he was the **Democratic minority leader** in the Senate in 1953, the **majority leader** in 1955, and then his party's presidential candidate. He lost to John Kennedy, and became his **vice-president** when Kennedy won the

1908
Born near Stonewall, Texas

1930
Graduates from Southwest Texas State Teachers College

1937
Elected to House of Representatives

1948
Elected to Senate

1953
Becomes Democratic leader in the Senate

1960
Runs for the presidency, and becomes vice-president to Kennedy

1963
Becomes president after assassination of Kennedy

election. One thousand days later, John Kennedy was assassinated, and Lyndon Johnson became the president of a saddened nation.

Johnson grabbed the opportunity to push changes through **Congress**. In 1964 Congress became overwhelmingly **Democrat**, which helped Johnson to get his new laws passed. He introduced Medicare – government-funded healthcare for the elderly, and the important *Civil Rights Act* and *Voting Rights Act*. He gave money to education and the arts, raised the **minimum wage**, and introduced laws to protect consumers and the environment. These **reforms** aimed to get rid of

▲ Johnson is sworn in as president as Jacqueline Kennedy looks on. They were aboard the plane that carried the body of John Kennedy back to Washington after his assassination.

THE VIETNAM WAR

☆ In 1954 the former French colony of Vietnam was divided between a Communist North and a pro-American South. North Vietnamese soldiers entered the South in order to take over the government and make the country Communist. President Kennedy sent the first US military advisors to South Vietnam in 1961. In 1964 Johnson asked Congress to allow him to wage war in Vietnam. The US had nearly 400,000 soldiers in Vietnam by 1966 and was dropping bombs on North Vietnam daily. The US eventually realized that it was not going to win the war. It withdrew US troops and signed a ceasefire in 1973.

poverty in the richest country in the world. Many Americans came to prosper in Johnson's new society. In 1964 Johnson ran for president and won the election with one of the biggest **landslides** in history.

VIETNAM

Johnson believed that **Communism** was a threat to the world. He sent thousands of soldiers to South Vietnam to prevent a Communist takeover. As the Vietnam War continued and the deaths mounted, people started to protest. Johnson's "Great Society" was soon overshadowed by the horrors of Vietnam. In 1968 Johnson was so unpopular with the American people that he decided not to run for president a second time and retired.

Five years later Johnson was dead. He was exhausted and disappointed that his reputation as a great reformer was destroyed by a war he could not win.

1964
Sends troops to Vietnam

1964
Elected in his own right to the presidency

1964
Civil Rights Act passed

1965
Civil Rights Voting Act passed

1968
Decides not to run again for president

1973
Dies near San Antonio, Texas

▶ Civil rights leader, Martin Luther King, Jr. inspired people with his speeches. He was assassinated in 1968.

1913
Born in
Yorba Linda,
California

1937
Gains law degree
from Duke
University

1942
Serves in
US Navy

1946
Elected to House
of Representatives

1950
Elected
to Senate

1952
Vice-president
to Eisenhower

1960
Loses presidential
election to
John Kennedy

1962
Loses election
for governor
of California

Richard Nixon is the first and only president who resigned while in office. He was distrusted and disliked before he became president and was disliked even more afterwards. He was, in many ways, a successful president, but in the end, his dishonesty let him down. Nixon was born in California and became a lawyer. After war service, he ran for the **House of Representatives**. Nixon claimed that one of the **Democrats** in the House supported **Communism** and won his place because he promised to fight Communists. He then became a member of the **Committee on Un-American Activities** and became famous for his prosecution of the supposed Communist spy, Alger Hiss.

In 1950 Nixon ran for the **Senate**. He criticized his opponent, Helen Douglas, and won again. Dwight Eisenhower chose Nixon as his **vice-presidential running mate**. But Nixon was charged with using **campaign** funds for himself during his Senate race, and he only won by appealing on television for support from the public. Nixon turned out to be a better vice-president than many people imagined. He supported **civil rights** but also wanted to increase

☆ **TERM**
1969–1974

☆ **PARTY**
Republican

☆ **VICE-PRESIDENTS**
*Spiro Agnew;
Gerald Ford*

☆ **FIRST LADY**
Thelma Ryan

☆ **STATES IN THE UNION** *50*

37th president

RICHARD NIXON

Well, I'm not a crook.

RICHARD NIXON, 1973

TRICKY DICK
Throughout his career, people had doubts about Richard Nixon's honesty. Long before Watergate, he was known as "Tricky Dick" Nixon.

1968 Elected president

1969 Apollo XI lands on the Moon

◀ In 1972 President Nixon made a historic visit to China, the first ever by a US president.

1972 Break-in at the Democratic HQ, Watergate Hotel

1972 Re-elected president

1973 Ceasefire ends US involvement in Vietnam War

I WANT OUT

1974 Resigns because of Watergate involvement

1994 Dies in New York City

◀ There were many US protests against the Vietnam War in the early 1970s.

America's influence abroad. When Eisenhower stepped down in 1960, Nixon fought John Kennedy for the presidency. He lost narrowly and then fought and lost an election to become governor of California. "You won't have Dick Nixon to kick around anymore," he snarled at the press, and many thought that his political career was over.

IN AND OUT OF POWER

But Nixon's career was not over. He rebuilt his reputation and, in 1968, narrowly won the presidential election. As president, he cut government spending and introduced anti-crime measures. In 1972 he signed a **treaty** with the USSR to reduce the number of weapons held by the two countries. Nixon also stopped the war in Vietnam, withdrew US troops, and turned the army into a volunteer force.

But Nixon trusted no-one except his closest advisers. Throughout his time in office, he used his power to bully people and bug telephones. Nixon was so keen to win re-election in 1972 that he used **dirty tricks** against the Democratic Party and its anti-war policies. These dirty tricks were made public when it was revealed that

▲ On July 24, 1969 Neil Armstrong became the first person to walk on the Moon. He said it was "one small step for man, one giant leap for mankind."

Nixon had secretly taped all his conversations in the White House. The evidence on the tapes ruined him. By this time, many of his advisers had resigned in disgrace, or faced criminal charges. Nixon himself would have to pay a huge bill for unpaid **taxes**.

Faced with all this, Nixon resigned rather than face **impeachment** by **Congress**. Nixon may not have been the first president to use dirty tricks against his opponents, but he was the first to get caught. This scandal along with his bad reputation meant that he left government in disgrace.

WATERGATE

☆ In June 1972 burglars broke into the headquarters of the Democratic National Committee at the Watergate Hotel in Washington. They were part of a dirty tricks campaign to stop the Democrats from winning the 1972 election. Evidence soon emerged that the dirty tricks campaign had been run from the White House. Many of Nixon's advisers were forced to resign. Nixon himself resigned in disgrace in August 1974.

Nixon announces his resignation

GERALD FORD

1913
Born in Omaha, Nebraska

☆ **TERM**
1974–1977

☆ **PARTY**
Republican

☆ **VICE-PRESIDENT**
Nelson Rockefeller

☆ **FIRST LADY**
Elizabeth "Betty" Bloomer

☆ **STATES IN THE UNION** *50*

> *Our long national nightmare is over… our great republic is a government of laws and not of men.*

GERALD FORD, 1974

Gerald Ford became president because of the resignation of Richard Nixon. **No one elected Ford to be president, just** as no one had previously elected him to be **vice-president**. He was the only person in US history to hold both offices without being elected to either. His time in office was short and unmemorable.

UNELECTED OFFICE

A keen sportsman, Gerald Ford practiced law and served in the US Navy during World War II before entering politics in 1948. For 15 years he was a competent **Republican** member of the **House of Representatives**. In 1965 Ford became the **minority leader** in the House for the Republican Party. He may have stayed in this post, but, in 1973, Spiro Agnew resigned from the office of vice-president and Ford took over the job.

Agnew was caught taking bribes and evading taxes, so he was forced to resign. By this time,

THE FORDS

☆ Gerald Rudolph Ford was born Leslie Lynch King. When he was three years old, his mother divorced his violent father and married a man called Gerald Rudolph Ford. Leslie Lynch King was later renamed and became the second Gerald Rudolph Ford. Ford did not learn about this until he was in his teenage years.

☆ Betty Ford was often outspoken. She publicized her breast cancer to help save people's lives. She also told the world that she was addicted to alcohol and painkillers, and she set up the Betty Ford Clinic to help other people overcome their addictions.

1931
Wins football
scholarship
to Michigan
University

1935
Sports coach at
Yale University

1941
Gains law
degree
from Yale

1942
Joins US
Navy

1948
Elected to
House of
Representatives

1965
Becomes
minority
leader of
the House

1973
Becomes
vice-president

1974
Becomes
president
when Nixon
resigns

1976
Defeated in
presidential
election by
Jimmy Carter

◀ President Ford pardons Richard Nixon on US television in 1973.

LEFT AND RIGHT Gerald Ford is left-handed when he sits down to eat or write, but is right-handed when he stands up to play sports.

President Nixon was losing popularity because of the growing number of allegations against him of corruption and **dirty tricks**. Nixon wanted a decent, competent person to be his vice-president. Gerald Ford was the perfect man – he was loyal to Nixon but, above all, he was honest and reasonably efficient. Eight months later, Richard Nixon resigned, and Ford became president.

CLEARING UP THE MESS

Ford took over the presidency when the US was experiencing many problems. The government was full of corruption, and few people had any respect for it or its politicians. The country was still divided after the Vietnam War and, in addition, it was suffering from a massive **economic depression** and high unemployment. Ford had an advantage because he was well liked and he was obviously a decent person, but he had little political experience for such a high position in government. As he said when he was sworn in as vice-president in 1973, "I am a Ford, not a Lincoln." It was unlikely that he could fix all the nation's problems as Abraham Lincoln had tried to do during the **Civil War**.

As if to prove that he was not up to the job, Ford's first act was to pardon Richard Nixon, which meant that Nixon would not have to face any criminal charges. Ford believed that the country should put the past behind it and look to the future, but many people were furious that Nixon was not being made to face justice for his crimes.

SOME SUCCESSES

Ford did have some successes as president. He continued Nixon's policy of co-operation with the USSR, and he met its leader, Leonid Brezhnev. Ford also managed to get the remaining US citizens out of South Vietnam without loss of life when the country was finally taken over by North Vietnam in 1975. He also took military action against Cambodia after it seized a US ship. But people still considered him as being tarnished because of his association with Richard Nixon.

Ford won his party's nomination to fight the 1976 election, but he was defeated by Jimmy Carter. This new man promised a different style of politics.

▶ The last American citizens and their families still living in South Vietnam at the end of the Vietnam War are evacuated from the roof of the US embassy in Saigon in 1975.

James "Jimmy" Carter was new to politics when he became president. He had never been vice-president, or a member of either of the Houses of **Congress**, unlike most of his predecessors. It was the fact that Carter was new that won him the office, but it was also for this reason that his term was not successful.

Jimmy Carter came from the Deep South, and he was the first president from that region since before the **Civil War**. He made his money in the peanut business and, as a **Democrat**, he rose through Georgian politics to become governor from 1971–75. By law, Carter could only serve one term as governor, so, once he was out of office, he turned his attention to the presidency.

No-one took him seriously, but Carter offered a style of politics that was almost anti-politics. He was religious, sincere, and honest and was not tainted in any way with the politics of Washington. In a close race with Gerald Ford, he won the 1976 election and arrived in Washington determined to make a change.

ALL CHANGE IN THE WHITE HOUSE

Carter immediately re-organized the government. He set up the post of energy secretary to deal with the energy crisis in the US, and pardoned the many men who had broken the law by refusing to fight in the Vietnam War. Abroad, he negotiated a **treaty** with Panama to return the US-controlled Panama Canal Zone to Panama's control by 2000. Carter also established good relations with China and continued to talk with USSR representatives about reducing the number of nuclear weapons in the two countries. Above all, he achieved what many thought was impossible by bringing together the

☆ **TERM**
1977–1981

☆ **PARTY**
Democrat

☆ **VICE-PRESIDENT**
Walter Mondale

☆ **FIRST LADY**
Rosalynn Smith

☆ **STATES IN THE UNION** *50*

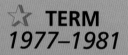

39th president

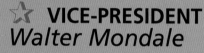

...at the end of this administration, we shall be able to stand up anywhere in the world and say "I'm a Georgian" and be proud of it.

JIMMY CARTER, 1971

1924
Born in Plains, Georgia

1946
Graduates from US Naval Academy in Annapolis

▲ In 1978 President Carter brought Menachem Begin of Israel (left) and Anwar Sadat of Egypt (right) together for peace talks. Since the foundation of Israel in 1948, the country had been in conflict with its Arab neighbors.

THE CARTER TEAM

Jimmy Carter was a relaxed president. At his inauguration, he got out of his car and walked some of the way to the White House in a show of openness. Jimmy and his wife, Rosalynn, were a real team, and she shared all his work problems. Every Thursday, they met for lunch to talk about the decisions that the president had to make in the next week.

leaders of Egypt and Israel which were at war with each other. After serious discussions, the two countries signed the Camp David Accords and Egypt agreed to recognize Israel in return for regaining its lost region of Sinai. A peace treaty between the two countries was signed in 1979. The Egyptian president, Anwar Sadat, and the Israeli prime minister, Menachem Begin, gained the **Nobel Peace Prize** for this historic reconciliation.

AN ULTIMATE FAILURE

As well as successes, Carter had failures. He was unknown in politics, so he found it difficult to get new laws through Congress. Unemployment and prices rose, and people did not believe that Carter could solve the country's economic problems.

In November 1979, a situation arose that ruined Carter's reputation. Iranian soldiers seized the US embassy in the country's capital city of Tehran, and held 52 US citizens hostage. The following year, a US secret mission failed to rescue them. For many Americans, it was a huge national shame that the strongest country in the world was being

held to ransom by a religious group in the Middle East. The Russian invasion of Afghanistan at Christmas 1979 added to the feeling that the US was losing its power in the world. As a result, Carter lost the 1980 presidential election by a **landslide** to the **Republican**, Ronald Reagan, who promised to restore American pride.

After leaving the White House, Carter retired home to Georgia. But, unlike other former presidents, he did not leave politics. He used his political experience to promote world peace. He acted as a negotiator between countries that were at war. He also oversaw elections in newly democratic countries and promoted human rights wherever he could. Over time, his reputation has grown, so that he is now more widely respected than he ever was as president.

▶ In 1978 Muhammad Ali won the world heavyweight boxing championship for the US for a record third time. He had won the title in 1964 and again in 1974.

BOOKED IN
The president's youngest child, Amy, was invited to state banquets in the White House. She was allowed to bring a book to read during the boring bits.

1953
Leaves US Navy to run father's peanut farm

1962
Elected to Georgia State Senate

1970
Elected governor of Georgia

1976
Elected president

1979
Israel and Egypt sign peace treaty

1980
Loses presidential election to Ronald Reagan

1981
Devotes himself to international peace-keeping

At 69 years old, Ronald Reagan was the oldest man to have been elected president. He was also the only president who had been divorced, the leader of a **trade union**, and a former film star. Reagan was one of the more successful US presidents, despite the many problems that arose during his presidency.

Ronald Reagan was born into a poor family in Illinois. As a teenager, he worked as a lifeguard during the summer, and later became a radio announcer. In 1937 Reagan was noticed by a Hollywood agent who took him to California, where he soon became a film star. Over the years, he featured in more than 50 movies. He became an important member of the Screen Actors Guild, the trade union for actors and he was the organization's president six times.

Reagan had grown up during the **Great Depression** and was a committed **Democrat** who believed in President Roosevelt's **New Deal**. But during the 1950s, he began to change his views. Reagan disliked the violence that he saw during a strike at the Warner Brothers studios and believed that **Communists** were influencing the movie industry. He thought that the Democratic Party was soft on **Communism**, so he became a **Republican** in 1962.

A RAPID ASCENT

In 1964 Reagan made a powerful speech in favor of Barry Goldwater, the Republican candidate for president. Goldwater lost the election to Lyndon Johnson, but Reagan still made his reputation with his presentation skills. Two years later he ran for governor of California and won easily. He promised to cut **taxes**, reduce government spending, and get tough on student protesters. In reality, his words were tougher than his policies, but he was a successful governor, and served for two terms. In 1968 and 1976, Reagan used his popularity to run for his party's presidential nomination. He finally won in 1980.

☆ **TERM**
1981–1989

☆ **PARTY**
Republican

☆ **VICE-PRESIDENT**
George Bush

☆ **FIRST LADY**
Nancy Davis

☆ *States in the Union 50*

TWO MRS. REAGANS
Ronald Reagan is the only president to have been divorced. In 1952, he divorced his first wife, the actress Jayne Wyman, to marry another actress, Nancy Davis.

40th president

RONALD REAGAN

1911
Born in Tampico, Illinois

1937
Appears in first Hollywood film

1947
Becomes president of the Screen Actors Guild

As president, Ronald Reagan offered the American people a new era of confidence in their country. He cut **taxes** and **welfare** spending. He also cut down the amount of government money spent on the environment and on **civil rights**. Reagan spent a lot of money on the armed services and weapons. This policy, known as "Reaganomics," cut **inflation** and unemployment and made the rich richer. But it also made the poor poorer and increased the government's debt to more than $200 billion, which was the highest it had been in US history.

Economically, Reagan's policy was not a great success, but it did revive the American people's confidence in their country and government. It also provided Reagan with a **landslide** victory when he ran for president again in 1984.

THE SECOND TERM

Reagan worked with the new leader of the USSR, Mikhail Gorbachev, to improve relations between the two countries. The two leaders met for talks four times and agreed to destroy some of their nuclear missiles. This was the first time that the number of nuclear weapons in the world had been reduced.

But then Reagan got involved in selling weapons to Iran. He did this in order to persuade Iran to put pressure on Islamic militants to release hostages that they were holding prisoner in Lebanon. He had previously called Iran one of the most "evil and murderous nations in the world."

USSR VERSUS USA

☆ President Reagan was afraid that the Communist USSR would attack the US, so he modernized the country's defenses. Under Reagan, the US began to develop the Strategic Defence Initiative (SDI), known as "Star Wars." This was a kind of shield in space, made from lasers, that would destroy any missiles coming towards the USA.

A "Star Wars" satellite

The money gained from Iran was then used illegally. It was given to revolutionaries who were trying to bring down the left-wing government of Nicaragua. When this information became known, Reagan's reputation was severely damaged. In 1989 Reagan stepped down as president. He left the US richer and more confident than before, but also left it with its biggest-ever debt. Many people still think Reagan is one of the most successful and likeable presidents in recent US history.

◀ In 1981 the world's first re-usable space shuttle flew back to Earth after 54 hours in space.

1962
Joins Republican Party

1966
Elected governor of California

1968 & 1976
Attempts to win nomination for presidency

1980
Elected president

1984
Re-elected president in biggest electoral victory in history

1989
Steps down as president

1994
Announces that he has Alzheimer's disease

▶ Reagan's term saw the start of the computer age. Millions of homes now have computers.

GEORGE BUSH

☆ **TERM**
1989–1993

☆ **PARTY**
Republican

☆ **VICE-PRESIDENT**
Dan Quayle

☆ **FIRST LADY**
Barbara Pierce

☆ **STATES IN THE UNION** *50*

FIRST BASE STAR

George Bush was the captain of Yale's baseball team and played at first base. He was good enough to be approached by a professional team and later kept his baseball glove in a drawer in the Oval Office.

> *Read my lips – no new taxes.*
>
> **GEORGE BUSH, 1988**

Few presidents have been as qualified as George Bush was to become president. He had been in the armed forces, had worked in industry, had served as a US **ambassador**, had run the CIA, and for eight years had been **vice-president**. His term saw many successes around the world, but his failures in the US meant that he only lasted one term.

George Bush was born into a rich **Republican** family and he had a privileged upbringing. His father was a US **senator** from Connecticut. As soon as he was 18, Bush joined the navy and became the youngest navy pilot in World War II, flying 58 missions. During one of these missions, he was shot down over the Pacific Ocean. Bush was rescued by a US submarine, and was awarded the Distinguished Flying Cross for his bravery. After the war, he studied law at Yale University. Bush then moved to Texas, where he set up a profitable oil development company.

INTO POLITICS

In 1966 George Bush was elected to the **House of Representatives** and served two terms. When he lost office in 1970, President Nixon appointed him US ambassador to the UN, and then chair of the Republican Party. Later, President Ford sent Bush to China – he was the first US representative to be posted to **Communist** China. On his return to the US, he ran the Central Intelligence Agency (CIA). He was now a major figure in the Republican Party.

1924
Born in Milton, Massachusetts

1942
Serves as fighter pilot in World War II

1948
Graduates from Yale University

1950
Sets up oil development company in Texas

1966
Elected to US House of Representatives

1971
US ambassador to the UN

1973
Chairs Republican Party

◄ Barbara Pierce supported her husband's career and moved with him to 17 different cities and 29 homes during their long and happy marriage.

In 1980 Bush lost the race to become the party's presidential candidate to Ronald Reagan. Bush became vice-president and, for eight years, was a loyal supporter.

PRESIDENT AT LAST

In 1988 George Bush got his chance. Ronald Reagan retired and Bush was elected president against the **Democrat**, Michael Dukakis. The election that the two men fought was one of the toughest in US history.

While Bush was in office, the **Cold War** came to an end. The USSR withdrew its troops from Afghanistan, which it had invaded in 1979, as well as from Eastern Europe. This allowed many revolutions to take place across the region. Communist governments were overthrown, the Berlin Wall came down, democratic elections were held for the first time, and East and West Germany were united as one country. In 1991 the USSR collapsed, and 15 new countries were created. Also in 1991, the US won a victory over Iraq and ended the Gulf War. As a result, Bush became one of the most popular presidents in history.

Although he achieved much abroad, Bush was less successful at home. When he was elected, he had promised not to raise **taxes**,

but he was forced to increase a range of taxes in 1990, in order to reduce the government's debt. Meanwhile, unemployment rose and the economy slowed down. Many people were also concerned that America was losing its powerful place in the world economy to Japan and other strong countries. Bill Clinton, Bush's Democratic challenger in 1992, used these fears about the weakness of the US economy to fight hard against Bush. Clinton won the presidential election and, after only one term in office, Bush was defeated.

THE GULF WAR

☆ On August 2, 1990 Iraqi armies invaded their small, neighboring state of Kuwait. Iraq wanted to capture this oil-rich state and gain better access to the Persian Gulf. The US and 29 other countries immediately sent troops into the region to recapture Kuwait. On January 17, 1991, US and other air forces began to bomb Baghdad, the Iraqi capital. The land invasion of Kuwait began on February 24. One hundred hours later, Iraq was defeated and Kuwait was free.

US troops in the Gulf War

1974
US ambassador to China

1976
Director of the CIA

1980
Fights for, but loses, presidential nomination to Ronald Reagan

1980
Becomes US vice-president under Reagan

1988
Elected president

1991
Sends US troops to the Gulf

1992
Loses presidential election to Bill Clinton

▶ The fall of the Berlin Wall in 1989 united the city of Berlin and led to the unification of Germany in 1990.

1946
Born in Hope, Arkansas

1968
Gains degree from Georgetown University, Washington, D.C.

1973
Gains law degree from Yale University

1976
Elected Arkansas state attorney

1978
Elected governor of Arkansas

1980
Loses governorship in election

1982
Regains governorship

At 46, William "Bill" Clinton was one of the youngest men to be elected president. During his two terms, the US economy was buoyant, but his presidency was marked by political failures and personal scandals.

Bill Clinton was born William Jefferson Blythe. His father died before he was born, and he was raised by his mother. She remarried and Bill took his step-father's surname. Clinton was a brilliant scholar. He studied at Georgetown University, then at Oxford University in Britain, and at Yale, gaining two degrees. He then returned to his home state of Arkansas and entered politics.

Clinton was determined to become president. In 1974 he tried for a seat in the **House of Representatives**, but failed. Two years later, he was elected **attorney general** of Arkansas. In 1978 at the age of 32, he was elected governor, the youngest in the state's history.

☆ **TERM**
1993–2001

☆ **PARTY**
Democrat

☆ **VICE-PRESIDENT**
Al Gore

☆ **FIRST LADY**
Hillary Rodham

☆ **STATES IN THE UNION** *50*

42nd president

WILLIAM CLINTON

There is nothing wrong with America that cannot be cured by what is right with America.

BILL CLINTON, 1993

NAME AFTER NAME
Bill Clinton revived his political career so many times after facing defeat that he is known as "the Comeback Kid." Clinton is also known as "Slick Willie," since he can argue both sides of an issue.

Clinton worked hard for peace in Northern Ireland.

Clinton tried to bring together the Israeli and Palestinian leaders to bring peace to the Middle East.

1992
Wins presidential election for Democrats

1996
Wins re-election

1999
Survives impeachment by Congress

2001
Steps down as president

THE COMEBACK

After his first term in office as governor, Clinton was not re-elected. He learned the lessons of this defeat and was re-elected in 1982, and a further four times. He made a name for himself and used it to run for the presidency in 1992. He campaigned as a New Democrat and easily defeated George Bush. Clinton's ideals were **Democrat** in terms of social policy, but closer to the **Republicans** in their support of big businesses and small government.

SUCCESSES AND FAILURES

As president, Clinton was fortunate that the US economy was in good shape. He presided over the USA's longest economic boom in history. More people had jobs than ever before, and new computer companies made many people rich. As a result, Clinton easily won re-election in 1996.

Clinton had many successes as president. But, in 1994, he tried to **reform** the healthcare system

IMPEACHMENT?

☆ Bill Clinton was the first president since Andrew Johnson in 1868 to face impeachment. In 1998 Clinton was accused of improper behavior. He denied the allegations at first. But, after a federal grand jury made an investigation, the special prosecutor, Kenneth Starr, recommended impeachment. The House of Representatives decided that Clinton was guilty of obstruction of justice and perjury (lying in court). The Senate disagreed and acquitted Clinton of the charges in 1999. Clinton was allowed to remain president.

FIRST LADY OF POLITICS

☆ Many people thought that Hillary Rodham would run for president herself, but she chose instead to support Bill in his political career. In 2000, she decided to run for election as senator for New York State. This is the first time in US history that a First Lady has run for elected office.

to provide good health cover for all Americans. The plan was promoted by the First Lady, Hillary Rodham Clinton, but was defeated in **Congress**. Then the Democrats lost control of both Houses of Congress to the Republicans for the first time since 1954. Clinton had to abandon many of his own policies and work with a hostile Congress. The two sides had many battles, which Clinton usually won. Then, in 1998, he was almost **impeached**, but the "Comeback Kid" survived even that ordeal.

Bill Clinton was a controversial president who attracted respect and hostility in equal measure. Despite the scandals that surrounded him, he ended his two terms as president as popular as ever, with the United States of America richer than at any time in its history.

ROAD TO THE WHITE HOUSE

The race to the White House is a long, difficult, and expensive contest. From start to finish, the race lasts well over a year, from when the candidates declare their intention to run for president to the final vote on election day. Many candidates give up along the way and there is only one winner – whoever becomes president.

Candidates need many millions of dollars to enter and survive the race. This money is raised from individual supporters, fund-raising events, big businesses, trade unions, and other organizations. Candidates also need teams of supporters that will work on their behalf to raise funds, send out letters and press releases, ask voters for their support, organize rallies and other events, and do many other tasks that make up a successful **campaign**.

The candidates themselves must make television broadcasts and commercials, and appear in shopping malls, schools, and town events across the country. They must keep up a tough schedule from morning until night, seven days a week. Above all, they must be seen to be "running to win."

STATE BY STATE

Throughout the year, from Iowa in January to New Jersey in June, candidates campaign in each of the 50 states of the **Union**. Each state has the right to send **delegates** to the political parties' national **Conventions** in proportion to its total population. The states with more people living in them have more delegates, so it is important for a candidate to win support in the bigger states. Candidates try to meet as many voters as possible.

CAUCUSES AND PRIMARIES

States vary in how they elect their delegates and each state has its own rules. Some states hold "caucuses" while most hold "primaries." A caucus is a private meeting that political party members have to attend to register their votes. These meetings take place in each voting precinct (area).

A primary is a state-wide election. In a primary, **Republican** and **Democrat** supporters, who are marked as supporters on the electoral roll, cast their votes for their favorite candidate. Most state

ELECTION 2000 TIMETABLE

In the race for the presidency, candidates declare themselves about one year before the election. This gives them time to set up their campaigns, raise money, and get themselves known across the country. In 1999 the Republican candidates were Governor George Bush of Texas, Arizona senator, John McCain, business executive, Steve Forbes, former diplomat, Alan Keyes, Senator Orin Hatch, and Congressman Gary Bauer. The Democratic candidates were Vice-President Al Gore and former New Jersey senator, Bill Bradley.

☆ JANUARY 24, 2000
The traditional starting place for a presidential election campaign is New Hampshire. In 2000 Iowa held its caucus first. Though not as important as a primary, the result of a caucus shows who is doing well and who is not. George Bush and Al Gore emerge victorious.

☆ FEBRUARY 2000
The first primary election is always held in New Hampshire. It is a small state and candidates meet many voters to listen to their concerns. John McCain defeats George Bush and leads the Republican race. Al Gore wins easily against Bill Bradley and leads the Democratic race. Defeated candidates begin to pull out. Bush then defeats McCain in the South Carolina Republican Primary and takes the lead. But McCain defeats Bush in Arizona (McCain's home state) and Michigan, and the Republican race heats up!

☆ MARCH 2000
Super Tuesday – 13 Republican and 15 Democratic primaries take place. Super Tuesday is designed to get the contest over with and select a candidate before the party conventions. Around 39 per cent of the national electorate can vote on Super Tuesday, which will choose around half of the total delegates to the two parties'

national conventions. After Super Tuesday, George Bush and Al Gore are the overwhelming winners. Bush has 1,068 delegates (1,034 are needed to win) while Gore has 2,497 delegates (2,169 are needed to win). Bradley and McCain retire from the race.

☆ JUNE 6, 2000
Last primary elections take place, but the result is not in doubt.

☆ JULY 31–AUGUST 3, 2000
The Republican National Convention selects Bush as its presidential candidate. Bush names Dick Cheney as his running mate.

☆ AUGUST 14–17, 2000
The Democratic National Convention selects Al Gore as candidate. He names Joseph Lieberman as his running-mate.

☆ SEPTEMBER 5, 2000
The proper campaign starts after Labor Day weekend.

☆ OCTOBER 2000
Televised debates are shown, between the two presidential and between the two vice-presidential candidates.

☆ NOVEMBER 7, 2000
Election day.

☆ DECEMBER 18, 2000
Electoral College voters meet in each state to elect their candidate.

☆ JANUARY 6, 2001
Congress counts the Electoral College votes to elect the president.

☆ JANUARY 20, 2001
Inauguration takes place for the 43rd president of the USA.

primaries only allow registered party supporters to vote, but some are open to supporters of all parties. In the primaries, the winning candidate gains the vote of all the state's party delegates. However, in the caucuses, delegates do not have to vote for that candidate and can decide themselves who to support at the Convention.

THE CONVENTION AND THE CAMPAIGN

Party delegates from each state attend their party's Convention to vote for their chosen candidate. The winning candidate gains the party's nomination for president. At the Convention, the candidate spells out his or her election promises and announces the **running mate** for **vice-president**. The election campaign between the two candidates and their running mates starts after Labor Day, which is always the first Monday in September. The candidates travel across the US, hold meetings, and make speeches. They also hold debates on television, which are important because more people watch the candidates on television than can ever meet them in the flesh.

THE ELECTION

The election is always held on the first Tuesday after the first Monday in November. On the day, the voters go to the polls across the US. The first results are announced within hours of the polls closing in the East Coast states. The winning candidate is usually announced within a day, but this did not happen in 2000. The number of votes in the state of Florida was so close that they had to be recounted. The final number of votes was debated so much that both sides took legal action to try to win the most votes. George W. Bush emerged victorious, and took his place as the 43rd president of the USA.

☆ **TERM**
2001–

☆ **PARTY**
Republican

☆ **VICE-PRESIDENT**
Dick Cheney

☆ **FIRST LADY**
Laura Welch

☆ **STATES IN THE UNION** *50*

43rd president

GEORGE W. BUSH

I kind of figure life is going to work its way out somehow.

GEORGE W. BUSH, 2000

SPORTS FAN
Like his father, George Bush played baseball for Yale. He never dreamt he would be president. "I just wanted to be Willie Mays," he said.

GLOSSARY

abolitionist A person who wants to get rid of slavery.

alliance A partnership between two or more countries.

ambassador A senior official of one country who represents that country abroad.

American Revolution *See entry for Revolutionary War.*

attorney general The chief law officer in the government who advises the president and Cabinet on legal matters.

ballot The act of voting where people mark crosses on paper to choose a party for election.

bill A proposal in Congress for a new law. Once a bill becomes law, it is known as an act.

Cabinet The group of ministers appointed by the president to run the country.

campaign Speeches, meetings, and other events held before an election to raise support in order to get a person elected.

campaigner A person who manages a campaign.

civil rights The personal rights of individual citizens in most countries, upheld by law.

civil service The government organization that administers public services in a country.

Civil War The war that broke out in America in 1861 when the slave-owning Confederate states left the Union.

Cold War The confrontation between the USA and the Communist USSR for domination of the world after 1945.

Colonial Army The army formed by the 13 colonies that fought for their independence from Britain from 1775 to 1781.

Committee on un-American Activities A committee that investigated activities by Communists and others that were thought to be anti-American. The investigation lasted from the 1930s until 1975.

Communism The belief in a society without social class in which all property is owned by the community.

Communist A person who supports Communism.

Confederacy The 11 southern states that left the Union during the Civil War.

Confederates Those who lived in the southern states during the Civil War. They had their own Congress at that time.

Congress The legislative, or law-making, body of the US. It is made up of the lower House of Representatives and the upper Senate.

Constitution A written document that sets out the political principles on which a country is founded and how its people are to be governed.

Constitutional Convention The meeting of politicians in 1787 during which the US Constitution was written.

Continental Congress The independent government of the 13 colonies that led the fight against the British and issued the Declaration of Independence in 1776. It first met in 1774 and was replaced by Congress under the new US Constitution in 1789.

convention The meeting of a political party held every four years to nominate its presidential and vice-presidential candidates.

D-Day Landings The invasion of German-occupied France in 1944 by the USA and its allies that led to the end of World War II in 1945.

Declaration of Independence The declaration made on July 4, 1776, by the 13 British colonies in North America that they were free from Britain.

delegate A person chosen or elected to represent their town, state, or political party at a conference or meeting.

Democrat A supporter of the Democratic Party.

Democratic Party A political party that first emerged under Andrew Jackson. It is one of the two big US political parties today.

Democratic-Republican The party of Thomas Jefferson, which believed in more power to individual states and a limited role for the federal government. It split in the 1820s into the Whigs and the Democrats.

depression *See under entry for economic depression.*

diplomat A person who represents his government.

dirty election/dirty tricks Underhand tactics, such as bugging phones and stealing private papers, designed to slander an opponent and win an election in an unfair way.

discrimination The unfair and unequal treatment of one group of people by another.

economic depression An economic slump or downturn in a country's wealth.

Electoral College The system of election that is used to elect the US president. *See page 6.*

establishment A ruling group of politicians, officials, business executives, and others who run a country.

federal A system of government where power is shared between national and state governments, with the states having a lot of power.

Federalist Party The party of George Washington and John Adams, which believed in a strong federal government. It was later replaced by the Democratic-Republican Party.

free state A state of the Union which has abolished slavery and allows people who have been slaves to be free.

French Revolution An uprising that broke out in France in 1789, and got rid of the royal family. A republic was set up by the revolutionaries in 1792.

Great Depression The worst economic depression in the US, which happened in the 1930s.

House of Representatives The lower House of Congress. Each state is represented in the House according to its population. Representatives are elected every two years.

impeachment A way of removing a president from office for wrong-doing. The House of Representatives hears the case and recommends impeachment to the Senate, which makes the decision on whether or not to keep the president. A two-thirds majority is needed to remove the president from office.

inauguration The official ceremony held when the new president and vice-president take up office.

Independent A politician who does not belong to any political party.

inflation A rise in prices for goods and services.

interventionist Someone who believes governments should get fully involved in a country's economy or society in order to make changes to it.

judiciary The judges, lawyers, and court system that organize the laws of the US.

kitchen cabinet A government team that is made up of the president's friends.

landslide An overwhelming victory, either in votes at an election, or in seats in Congress.

legislature A group of elected people that make laws. The US legislature is Congress.

Louisiana Purchase An area of land west of the Mississippi River which was bought by the US from the French in 1803.

majority leader The leader of the biggest political party in either House of Congress.

militia A group of civilians who carry arms and fight if there is a national emergency.

minimum wage The lowest salary that an employer can pay a worker as set out by the law.

minority leader The leader of the opposition, or smaller, party in the Houses of Congress.

Missouri Compromise *See page 19.*

Monroe Doctrine *See page 19.*

motion A formal proposal that is discussed and voted on in a debate or a meeting.

national debt The money borrowed by the government from banks and other countries in order to pay for the costs of running the country.

New Deal The name of Franklin Roosevelt's package of financial and economic reforms of 1933. *See page 71.*

Nobel Peace Prize An annual prize given to the person who has worked most for world peace. It was set up by Alfred Nobel, a Swedish chemist who invented dynamite.

North Atlantic Treaty Organization (NATO) A group of western European and North American countries set up to protect each of its members from attack by the USSR.

oath of office The promise made by a president when he takes office to act honestly, lawfully, and for the best interests of his country.

patronage Giving a political or administrative job to a person in order to gain their support.

political machine *See under entry for state machine.*

progressive candidate Someone who believes in major reform, or changes, within a country, which will have far-reaching effects on its citizens.

Reconstruction The program of reform and rebuilding of the southern states at the end of the Civil War. *See page 43.*

reform A change or changes in government policy, usually of benefit to a country's citizens.

republic A country, like the US, governed by an elected head of state called a president.

Republican Party A political party formed in 1854 by a group of Whigs and Democrats who were against slavery. Abraham Lincoln was its first president. It is one of the two big US political parties today.

Republican A supporter of the Republican Party.

Revolutionary War The war between the 13 American colonies and their British rulers from 1775 to 1783, which led to the independence of the US.

running mate The person chosen by a presidential candidate to campaign for the office of vice-president.

secession When one state or part of a country declares its independence from the rest of the country, as the Confederacy did when it left the Union in 1861.

secretary of commerce The US Cabinet member responsible for business affairs and trade.

secretary of state The US Cabinet member responsible for relations with other countries.

segregation A legal policy to separate different ethnic groups. This law was used in the South before the Civil War to keep African-American and white US citizens apart.

Seminole Nation Native Americans who lived in Florida.

Senate The upper house of Congress, made up of two senators or representatives from each state in the Union. It has 100 members. *See also state assembly.*

Senator A member of the Senate.

slavery Owning a person against their will so that they have no freedom or civil rights.

solicitor general A senior legal officer of the government just below the attorney general.

state assembly The law-making body of an individual state. Forty-nine out of 50 states have a state assembly that is similar to Congress.

state machine A strong political party that uses its large membership and good organization to control the city, state, or national government of a country. *See pages 24–25.*

state senate *See under entry for state assembly.*

Supreme Court The highest court of the US, which decides major constitutional and other complex cases. Its chief justice and eight other judges are appointed by the president and approved by the Senate.

tariff A tax on goods imported from other countries. Tariffs are meant to reduce the number of goods bought from overseas by encouraging people to buy home-grown products.

tax A payment collected by the government from individual people or companies. Workers' salaries, companies' profits, and some goods are all taxed.

trade union A group of workers set up to protect their rights and fight for better working conditions or pay.

treaty A formal agreement between two or more countries.

truce An agreement, usually temporary, between two or more countries or armies to stop fighting each other.

two-party political system A political system, such as in the USA, where two political parties dominate politics.

Union The 50 states of the US.

vice-president The deputy to the president who takes over if he resigns or dies. The first three vice-presidents were the runners-up in the presidential election, but he or she is now the president's running mate and a member of the his party.

welfare A system of financial and other assistance set up by governments for people in need.

Whig Party A political party set up to oppose the Democratic Party. It elected its first president, William Harrison, in 1840. The party split up over the subject of slavery and many of its members joined the Democrats or the Republicans in the 1850s.

INDEX

ACKNOWLEDGMENTS

PICTURE CREDITS Bite Communications Limited 87bc; **Corbis** 47tl, 77bl, 87cr; AFP 89tl, 91cl; Bettmann 21tr, 33br, 35tr, 44tc, 56bc, 71tr, 79bc, 83tl, 83br, 85tl, 90bc; Owen Franken 89bc; Wally McNamee 88tc, 91tc, 91cr; Reuters NewMedia Inc. 81br, 91tl; Peter Turnley 89cr; Underwood & Underwood 65cr; **Robert Harding Picture Library** Jonathan Hodson 2; Liaison International 53bc; **Peter Newark's American Pictures** 2c, 3c, 5bc, 6–7 (background),

10–11, 12–13, 14–15, 16–17, 18–19, 20c, 20br, 21bl, 22–23, 24–25, 26–27, 28–29, 30–31, 32tc, 33tr, 33bl, 34tc, 34br, 35bl, 36–37, 38–39, 40–41, 42–43, 44br, 45tl, 45bc, 46bc, 47cr, 48–49, 50–51, 52c, 53bl, 54–55, 57tl, 57tr, 57cl, 58–59, 60–61, 62–63, 64bc, 65tl, 65br, 66–67, 68–69, 70tc, 70bc, 71tl, 71bc, 72–73, 74–75, 76bc, 77tl, 77br, 78tc, 79cr, 80bc, 81tl, 81tr, 81bl, 82tc, 84bc, 85bc, 86bc, 87tl, 87br; **Popperfoto** Reuters/Jeff Mitchell 93bc

FRONT COVER Associated Press Danny Johnston bc; **Robert Harding Picture Library** Jonathan

Hodson tc; **Peter Newark's American Pictures** tl, tr, bl, br

Every effort has been made to acknowledge correctly and contact the source of each picture. Two-Can apologises for any unintentional errors or omissions which will be corrected in future editions of this book.

Key t = top; b = bottom; c = center; l = left; r = right

Picthall and Gunzi Ltd would like to thank everyone involved in the production of this book and Tristan Binns, Bobbi Hernandez, and Barnaby Harward for much appreciated editorial assistance.

JEAN DE BRUNHOFF

BABAR
THE KING

Translated from the French by Merle S. Haas

Random House — New York

This title was originally cataloged by the Library of Congress as follows:
De Brunhoff, Jean   Babar the king; trans. from the French by Merle S. Haas.
Random House c1935
unp   col   illus   1 Elephants—Stories   2 Picture books for children   I. Title E
ISBN 0-394-80580-1 (trade); 0-394-90580-6 (lib. bdg.)

Printed in the United States of America   53 54 55 56 57 58 59 60

Off in the country of the elephants King Babar and Queen
Celeste are rejoicing: they have signed a treaty of peace with
the rhinoceros, and their friend, the Old Lady, has consented
to remain with them. She often tells the elephants' children
stories; her little monkey, Zephir, perched up in a tree, also
listens.

Leaving the Old Lady with Queen Celeste, Babar has gone for a walk along the banks of a large lake with Cornelius, the oldest and wisest of all the elephants, and he says to him, "This countryside is so beautiful that I would like to see it every day

as I wake up. We must build our city here. Our houses shall be on the shores of the lake, and shall be surrounded with flowers and birds." Zephir, who has followed them, would like to catch a butterfly he sees . . . .

While chasing the butterfly, Zephir meets his friend Arthur, the young cousin of the King and Queen, who was amusing himself hunting for snails. All of a sudden they see one, two, three, four dromedaries . . . five, six, seven dromedaries . . . eight, nine, ten . . . . There are more than they can count. And the chief of the cavalcade calls to them: "Can you please tell us where we can find King Babar?"

Escorted by Arthur and Zephir, the dromedaries have found Babar. They are bringing him all his heavy baggage and all the things which he had bought out in the big world, during his honeymoon. Babar thanks them: "You must be tired, gentlemen. Won't you rest under the shade of the palm trees?" Then, turning to the Old Lady and to Cornelius, he says: "Now we will be able to build our city."

Having called an assembly of all the elephants, Babar climbs up on a packing case and, in a loud voice, proclaims the following words: "My friends, I have in these trunks, these bales, and these sacks, gifts for each of you. There are dresses, suits, hats and materials, paint boxes, drums, fishing tackle and rods, ostrich feathers, tennis rackets and many other things. I will divide all this among you as soon as we have finished building our city. This city—the city of the elephants — I would like to suggest that we name Celesteville, in honor of your Queen."

All the elephants raised their trunks and cried: "What a good idea! What an excellent idea!"

8

The elephants set to work quickly. Arthur and Zephir hand out the tools. Babar tells each one what he should do. He marks with sign-boards where the streets and houses should go. He orders some to cut down trees, some to move stones; others saw wood or dig holes. With what joy they all strive to do their best! The Old Lady is playing the phonograph for them and from time to time Babar plays on his trumpet; he is fond of music. All the elephants are as happy as he is. They drive nails, draw logs, pull and push, dig, fetch and carry, opening their big ears wide as they work.

Over in the big lake the fish are complaining among themselves: "We can't even sleep peacefully any longer," they say. "These elephants make the most dreadful noise! What are they building? When we jump out of the water we really haven't time to see clearly. We'll have to ask the frogs what it is all about."

The birds also gathered together to discuss what the elephants were up to. The pelicans and the flamingos, the ducks and the ibis and even the smaller birds all twittered, chirrupped and quacked, and the parrots enthusiastically kept repeating: "Come and see Celesteville, the most beautiful of all cities! Come and see Celesteville, the most beautiful of all cities!"

Here is Celesteville! The elephants have just finished building it and are resting or bathing. Babar goes for a sail with Arthur and Zephir. He is well satisfied, and admires his new capital. Each elephant has his own house. The Old Lady's is at the

upper left, the one for the King and Queen is at the upper right. The big lake is visible from all their windows. The Bureau of Industry is next door to the Amusement Hall which will be very practical and convenient.

Today Babar keeps his promise. He gives a gift to each elephant and also serviceable clothes suitable for work-days and beautiful rich clothes for holidays. After thanking their King most heartily, the elephants all go home dancing with glee.

Babar has decided that next Sunday all the elephants will
dress up in their best clothes and assemble in the gardens
of the Amusement Park. The gardeners have much to do.
They rake the paths, water the flower beds and set out the
last flower pots.

The elephant children are planning a surprise for Babar and Celeste. They have asked Cornelius to teach them the song of the elephants. Arthur had the idea. They are very attentive, keep time, and will know it perfectly by Sunday.

SONG OF THE ELEPHANTS

MELODY

Pa- ta- li di- ra- pa- ta crom- da crom- da ri- pa- lo

REFRAIN:

Pa- ta Pa- ta ko ko ko ------

WORDS

1st VERSE

PATALI DIRAPATA
CROMDA CROMDA RIPALO
PATA PATA
KO KO KO

2nd VERSE

BOKORO DIPOULITO
RONDI RONDI PEPINO
PATA PATA
KO KO KO

3rd VERSE

EMANA KARASSOLI
LOUCRA LOUCRA PONPONTO
PATA PATA
KO KO KO

NOTE: This song is the old chant of the Mammoths.
Cornelius himself doesn't know what the words mean —

The cooks are hurriedly preparing cakes and dainties of all kinds. Queen Celeste comes to help them. Zephir comes too, with Arthur. He tastes the vanilla cream to see if it is just right; first he puts in his finger, then his hand, and then his arm. Arthur is dying of envy and would like to stick his trunk in it.

In order to have one last taste Zephir bends his head, sticks out his tongue and *plouf!*—in he falls head first. At this sound the chief cook looks around and, greatly annoyed, fishes him out by the tail. The soup chef bursts out laughing. Arthur hides. Poor little Zephir is a sight, all yellow and sticky. Celeste scolds him and goes off to clean him up.

Sunday comes at last. In the gardens of the Amusement Park
the elephants saunter about dressed magnificently. The children
have sung their song, Babar has kissed each one. The cakes

were delicious! What a wonderful day! Unfortunately, it is over all too soon. The Old Lady is already organizing the last round of hide-and-seek.

The next day after their morning dip in the lake, the children go to school. And they are glad to find their dear teacher, the Old Lady, waiting for them. Lessons are never tiresome when she teaches.

After having settled the little ones at their tasks, she turns

her attention to the older ones, and asks them: "Two times
two?" — "Three," answers Arthur. "No, no, four," said
his neighbor Ottilie. "For, that's what we study for," sang
Zephir. "Four," repeated Arthur. "I'll not forget that
again, teacher."

All the elephants who are too old to attend classes, have chosen a trade. For example: Tapitor is a cobbler, Pilophage an officer, Capoulosse is a doctor, Barbacol a tailor, Podular a sculptor and Hatchibombotar is a street cleaner. Doulamor is a musician, Olur is a mechanic, Poutifour a farmer, Fandago is a learned man. Justinien is a painter and Coco a clown. If Capoulosse has holes in his shoes, he brings them to Tapitor, and, if Tapitor is sick, Capoulosse takes care of him. If Barbacol wants a statue for his mantelpiece, he asks Podular to carve one for him, and when Podular's coat is worn out Barbacol makes a new one to order for him. Justinien paints a portrait of Pilophage, who will protect him against his enemies. Hatchibombotar cleans the streets, Olur repairs the automobiles, and, when they are all tired, Doulamor plays his cello to entertain them. After having settled grave problems, Fandago relaxes and eats some of Poutifour's fruits. As for Coco, he keeps them all laughing and gay.

At Celesteville, all the elephants work in the morning, and in the afternoon they can do as they please. They play, go for walks, read and dream . . . . Babar and Celeste like to play tennis with Mr. and Mrs. Pilophage.

Cornelius, Fandago, Podular and Capoulosse prefer to play bowls. The children play with Coco, the clown. Arthur and Zephir have put on masks. There is a shallow pool in which to sail their boats and there are many other games besides.

But what the elephants like best of all

is the theater in the Amusement Park.

Every day, early in the morning, Hatchibombotar sprinkles the streets with his motor sprinkler. When Arthur and Zephir meet him, they quickly take off their shoes, and run after the car, barefoot. "Oh, what a fine shower!" they say laughingly. Unfortunately, Babar caught them at it one day. "No dessert for either of you, you rascals!" he cried.

Arthur and Zephir are mischievous, as are all little boys, but they are not lazy. Babar and Celeste visit the Old Lady, and are amazed to hear them play the violin and cello. "It is wonderful!" says Celeste, and Babar adds: "My dear children, I am indeed pleased with you. Go to the pastry shop and select whatever cakes you like."

Arthur and Zephir are very happy to have had all the cakes they wanted, but they are even more delighted when at the distribution of prizes, they hear Cornelius read out: "First prize for music: a tie between Arthur and Zephir." Very proudly, with wreaths on their heads, they went back to their seats. After having rewarded the good scholars, Cornelius made a noble speech.

". . . And now I wish you all a pleasant holiday!" he ended up. Everyone clapped hard and applauded loudly. Then, quite weary, he sat down, but alas and alack, his fine hat was on the chair and he crushed it completely. "A regular pancake!" said Zephir. Cornelius was aghast, and sadly looked at what was left of his hat. What would he wear on the next formal occasion?

The Old Lady promises Cornelius to sew some plumes on his old derby, and in order to console him further, she invites him to go for a ride on the new merry-go-round which Babar has just had built.

Podular has carved the animals, Justinien has painted them, and the motor was installed by Olur. All three of them are very skillful. They have also made the King's mechanical horse. Olur has just oiled it and Babar is winding it up. He wants to give it a final trial before the big celebration on the anniversary of the founding of Celesteville.

The weather is perfect the day of the celebration. Arthur marches at the head of the parade with Zephir and the band. Cornelius follows, his hat

completely transformed. Then come the soldiers and the trades companies. All those who are not marching are watching this unforgettable spectacle.

1.

On his way home from the celebration Zephir notices a curious stick.

2.

He goes to pick it up. Horrors! It is a snake which rears its head and hisses,

3.

and cruelly bites the Old Lady who tries to hide Zephir in her arms.

4.

Arthur furiously smashes his bugle on the snake's back and kills it.

The Old Lady's arm swells rapidly, and she hastens to the hospital.

Dr. Capoulosse takes care of her, and gives her a hypodermic of serum.

Zephir sadly remains near his mistress. She is very ill.

"I can't tell you until tomorrow whether she will get well," Capoulosse says to Babar.

As Babar leaves the hospital, he hears cries of "Fire! Fire!"
Cornelius' house is on fire. The stairway is already full of
smoke; the firemen succeed in rescuing Cornelius, but he
is half suffocated and a burning beam has injured him.
Capoulosse, summoned in great haste, gives him first-aid
before having him moved to the hospital. A match which
Cornelius thought he had thrown into the ashtray but
which had actually fallen, still lighted, in the trashbasket,
had been enough to start this terrible fire.

That night when Babar goes to bed, he shuts his eyes but
cannot sleep. "What a dreadful day!" he thinks. "It began
so well. Why did it have to end so badly? Before these two
accidents we were all so happy and peaceful at Celesteville!

"We had forgotten that misfortune existed! Oh my dear old Cornelius, and you, dear Old Lady, I would give my crown to see you cured. Capoulosse was to telephone me any news. Oh! How long this night seems, and how worried I am!"

. . . .

Babar finally drops off to sleep, but his sleep is restless and soon *he dreams:* He hears a knocking on his door. Tap! Tap! Tap! Then a voice says to him: "It is I, Misfortune, with some of my companions, come to pay you a visit." Babar looks out of the window, and sees a frightful old woman surrounded by flabby ugly beasts. He opens his mouth to shout: "Ugh! Faugh! Go away quickly!" But he stops to listen to a very faint noise — *Frr! Frr! Frr!* — as of birds flying in a flock, and he sees coming toward him . . .

. . . graceful winged elephants who chase Misfortune away from Celeste-ville and bring back Happiness. At this point he awakes, and feels ever so much better.

GOODNESS

FEAR

DESPAIR

INDOLENCE

MISFORTUNE

SICKNESS

ANGER

STUPIDITY

DISCOURAGEMENT

Babar dresses and runs to the hospital. Oh joy! What does he see? His two patients walking in the garden. He can hardly believe his eyes. "We are all well again," says Cornelius, "but all this excitement has made me as hungry as a wolf. Let's get some breakfast, and then later we'll rebuild my house."

A week later, in Babar's drawing room, the Old Lady says to her two friends: "Do you see how in this life one must never be discouraged? The vicious snake didn't kill me, and Cornelius is completely recovered. Let's work hard and cheerfully and we'll continue to be happy."

And since that day, over in the elephant's country, everyone has been happy and contented.